MW00332476

JUST THINK

Philosophy Puzzles for Children
Aged 9 to 90

Philip West

First published by Courthouse Press, 2020
https://just-think.net

Copyright © Philip West (2020)

ISBN: 978 1 8381692 0 6

All rights reserved. Except for brief quotations in critical articles or reviews, no part of this book may be reproduced in any manner without prior permission from the publisher.

The rights of Philip West as author have been asserted in accordance with the Copyright, Designs and Patents Act 1988.

Unless stated, all images are downloaded from https://pixabay.com. The Pixabay Licence: free for commercial use; no attribution required.

All correspondence should be directed to the author at philipwestauthor@gmail.com

Cover design by Jane Dixon-Smith

Printed by Amazon KDP Print

READ THIS FIRST

Is the world we see around us really there?
Is it ever right to do something wrong?
Should everyone be paid the same?
Is beauty just a matter of opinion?
Are miracles possible?

If you find questions like these fascinating, you are a philosopher. And if you are a philosopher, this book is for you.

The book contains thirty puzzles just like the ones above. You can do them in any order, so just pick one you like the look of and start right there.

Each puzzle starts with an argument between Philip and Phoebe, the terrible twins. This brother and sister rarely agree about anything, and both are always sure they are right. Sometimes only one of them is correct, but usually they are both partly right and partly wrong. Read their argument, think about their disagreement, and make up your own mind.

Then turn to the discussion section on the following page. This tells you what famous philosophers have said about the puzzle in the past. You may or may not agree with them. Then there are three tricky questions with which to test your friends, family and teachers, and websites to look at for more research.

There is a dedicated website for the book at https://just-think.net. Here you will find other puzzles, and you can submit answers to these if you want to.

A warning: unlike maths and science, philosophy is not a subject with clear-cut correct answers. Philosophers rarely agree with each other – just about the only agreed thing in philosophy is that philosophers disagree! If you would find this annoying, put the book down at once and do something else. But if you would love it – dive right in.

CONTENTS

iii

ALSO BY PHILIP WEST

Think Again: More Philosophy Puzzles for Children Aged 9 to 90 (2021) ISBN: 978 1 8381692 1 3

A companion volume to *Just Think*, this book contains thirty more puzzles divided into sections on ethics, language & epistemology, social & political philosophy, philosophy of science, aesthetics and logic.

The Old Ones in the Old Book: Pagan Roots of the Hebrew Old Testament (2012) ISBN 978 1 78099 171 9

The Hebrew scriptures reached their final form at the hands of monotheists. But they are the edited forms of much earlier stories, bearing witness to Israelite religion as practised before 600 BCE. This religion was a fascinating polytheistic paganism, close to the religion of the surrounding Canaanites. Written for adult non-specialists, this book is recommended for anyone interested in the early history of religious ideas.

INTRODUCTION FOR PARENTS AND TEACHERS

Some history

The origins of this book can be traced to 2006 when I was teaching at Westminster Under School in London. Every Friday morning, I would stand up in assembly and present a Philosopher of the Week puzzle to 300 boys aged 7 to 13. The puzzle was framed as an argument between two characters whimsically named Ludwig and Friedrich (after Ludwig Wittgenstein and Friedrich Nietzsche), and the students would have until the following Tuesday to post a solution in a box strategically placed outside my classroom door.

I was staggered by the interest and response which this initiative stirred up. The problem would be discussed in the playground and in the staff room, at home and on the bus, and by those of all ages. Every Tuesday my box would be filled with answers from students of all ages, plus quite a few from the staff as well. These formed the basis of another presentation at assembly, with the award of a tube of Smarties and a certificate to the winner. This went on most weeks for the best part of two years.

When I retired from teaching, the idea was taken up by an educational magazine aimed at bright and inquisitive 8 to 13-year-olds. The puzzle was renamed Just Think, and the argumentative characters morphed into Philip and Phoebe the terrible twins, but the idea was the same. The twins would fall out over some important issue, each of them apparently having unbeatable arguments on their side. A commentary followed, showing how the problem had been handled in philosophy. Then some extra questions were supplied for discussion with family and friends. In total, some fifty such articles were published between 2008 and 2018.

And there the story might have ended. But during the 2020 coronavirus lockdown, my son Mark revived the puzzles in the context of FUNdays Club, his after school and holiday club business based in Wiltshire. Mark would publish an adapted version of one of the puzzles and then hold an online discussion with a group of interested year 6 students. He reported it a big hit, and it was this which prompted me to try for a wider audience in the form of this book. I hope you find it as much fun as the earlier recipients of the puzzles.

Like many people, I came to an appreciation of philosophy rather late. Having left school a budding chemist, and after a formative year with VSO in West Africa, I was transformed into a biologist while studying Natural Sciences at Cambridge University. A brief career in science teaching followed, supplemented by a theology degree at King's College, London and then a PhD back at Cambridge. It was during this second stint at Cambridge that I was transfixed by philosophy. Starting with Descartes and Hume, and working through German philosophy via Kant, Hegel, Marx and Nietzsche, I eventually hit upon the 20th Century German philosopher and social theorist Jürgen Habermas, on whom I wrote my thesis. My love of philosophy and its questions has never deserted me since, even though I have largely earned my living teaching physics, chemistry and biology.

So, this book is dedicated to the past students of Westminster Under School and to my son Mark West. And, of course, to Nietzsche and Wittgenstein, with thanks for the loan of their names.

Who is this book for?

This book is aimed at intelligent, inquisitive young people, especially those aged 9 to 14, and their parents and teachers. The questions it deals with are of universal interest, however, and the subtitle 'Philosophy Puzzles for Children Aged 9 to 90' is not far wide of the mark.

The puzzles can be used in different ways. They can be read and thought about by a single person. But they come to life through argument, so discussing them in a group will be even more rewarding. This might be among friends, or within a family, or in a more formal classroom setting with a teacher and a class. In the last two cases, the Commentary at the back of the book should help adults guide the discussion to maximum effect.

The book is definitely not for people who like neat, cut-and-dried answers such as you find in maths and science, however. About the only agreed answer in philosophy is that philosophers always disagree! If a child would find that stimulating and exhilarating, if they are the sort of person who loves disagreeing with others, then this book is definitely for them.

What is philosophy?

The name "philosophy" comes from two Greek words: *philos* (liking or loving) and *sophos* (wisdom). So I suppose you could say that philosophy is "the love of wisdom". But that is of limited help – because who claims to dislike wisdom?

What philosophers really do is step back from activities, experiences and arguments and consider *how* people reach the conclusions they do. For example:

- Rather than asking 'What is the right thing to do in this situation?' they ask, 'How should people go about working out right and wrong in any situation?'

- Rather than asking 'Is that shimmering image really an oasis in the desert?' they ask, 'How do we ever know what is really out there in the world beyond our heads?'

- Rather than asking 'Is that a beautiful picture?' they ask, 'What is beauty anyway, and what makes anything beautiful or ugly?'

In other words, philosophy is about looking for deep patterns in the ways in which we live in the world.

Philosophy, unlike most disciplines, can be applied to any human activity or subject whatsoever. Most disciplines are defined by their subject matter. Biology, for example, is the study of living things, whereas geology is the study of rocks, and sociology is the study of

3

societies. But you can have a philosophy of biology, and a philosophy of geology, and a philosophy of sociology – in each case looking at how the professionals in these areas go about their work. This makes philosophy the study of everything (if you are a fan) or of nothing (if you are not). It is either the most important way of thinking in the whole world, or it is completely irrelevant and empty. And there are philosophers who argue for both these points of view.

How to use this book

Each puzzle in the book is self-contained. So a young person can look through the contents pages, pick a puzzle that interests them, and dive right in there. However, the puzzles are divided into sections, each dedicated to one of the major subdivisions of the subject, with a short introduction mainly for parents and teachers.

Each puzzle starts with an argument between Philip and Phoebe, the terrible twins, who are a fictional brother and sister. The positions they take up are persuasive – they both have one or more good arguments on their side. A discussion section follows, which explains how one or more famous philosophers have dealt with the puzzle in the past. Then there are three related questions, followed by one or more websites for optional research.

At the back of the book is a commentary, with a separate section for each puzzle. This is mainly intended for teachers who will be leading discussions on the puzzles, or for parents looking for a little more philosophical background.

Website and contact

There is a dedicated website for the book at https://just-think.net. Here the reader will find extra puzzles, and the opportunity to submit answers to these if they want to.

You can contact the author with questions or comments at philipwestauthor@gmail.com.

4

A: KNOWING THINGS

Can we know anything at all about the world around us and, if so, how do we know it? These are the questions tackled by the branch of philosophy called **epistemology**.

Philosophers disagree about the answers to both questions:

- **Sceptics** think we can know nothing at all for certain.

- **Empiricists** think we only find truth by using our senses – sight, hearing, touch, smell and taste.

- **Rationalists** think we find truth by using reason – by thinking.

We shall find examples of each type of philosopher in the pages that follow. Time to dive in and meet them!

1. Zhuangzi and the butterfly

The other day, Phoebe was reading this story in a book of Chinese philosophy:

> Once upon a time a Chinese philosopher called Zhuangzi, tired out from all his thinking, sat down in his garden in the warm sun and started to doze. Soon he was fast asleep and dreaming.
>
> He dreamed he was a beautiful butterfly, visiting flowers in the sunlit garden and sucking their nectar. Eventually, he grew tired from all his flying, so he settled down on a nice green leaf in the warm sun and started to doze.
>
> Soon he was fast asleep and dreaming. He dreamed he was a human philosopher called Zhuangzi, sitting in his garden.
>
> Zhuangzi woke up feeling really confused. He did not know who he was! Was he really the human philosopher Zhuangzi who had dreamed of being a butterfly? Or was he really a butterfly dreaming about being Zhuangzi?

'Silly man!' said Philip. '*I* never get confused about whether I'm dreaming or not. Dreams are totally different to real life.'

'No, they aren't,' retorted Phoebe. 'I often can't tell I'm dreaming until I wake up. Anyway, how can you be sure you aren't dreaming at the moment? Maybe you'll wake up in a minute and you'll still be tucked up in bed!'

'Right! So, I suppose you can't tell whether this room is real or not? It looks real enough to me. See! If you tap the walls, they're solid.'

'Maybe not,' said Phoebe thoughtfully. 'Perhaps the room is just part of my dream. If so, when I wake up it'll disappear.'

'Sisters!' muttered Philip in despair, wandering off to play with his computer.

6

Who is right, Philip or Phoebe?

Is there any way you can be *absolutely sure* you are not dreaming at the moment?

Is there any way you can be *absolutely sure* the world you see around you is real?

When you have thought about this problem carefully, turn to the next page.

Can we be sure the world we see around us is real?

Phoebe is right, of course – sometimes our dreams are very real, and we only realise they are dreams when we wake up. So, how do you know you are not dreaming right now?

The French philosopher **René Descartes** famously thought about this problem in a work called *Meditations*, published in 1641.

Descartes was unhappy with earlier attempts at philosophy because, he said, they do not give us certainty. He wanted to find things we can be absolutely sure about, not things which only *might* be true. Completely certain truths, he said, are ones which cannot even be doubted. Anything which we can doubt is not good enough – because it might be true, but it might not.

Descartes first considered the information we get through our senses: sight, hearing, touch, taste and smell. Can we be certain about this information? No, he decided, it can be doubted for three reasons:

- Our senses sometimes deceive us – think about optical illusions and mirages – and you can never absolutely trust anything once you know it can play tricks on you.

- It is impossible to be completely sure I am not dreaming at the moment. There is no absolutely fool proof test which tells me when I am awake.

- The world might be ruled by an evil demon, out to deceive me, who can make me see things which are not really there.

Our sense experience cannot be trusted, Descartes concluded. So, maybe the real world is nothing at all like it appears to me? Or maybe it isn't even there at all?

However, the fact that I am thinking about this problem means that *I* must exist. Why? Because even an evil demon cannot deceive me *if I am not here to deceive*. As he put it in a famous statement: '**I think, therefore I am.**'

8

Descartes was pretty sure he was awake when he wrote this. Like us, he knew that dreams are often more vague than real life, do not usually involve feeling pain or other sensations, and sometimes have weird plots. But, he said, "pretty sure" is not the same as "certain".

So, Phoebe is right, and Philip is wrong – at least according to Descartes.

A portrait of René Descartes (1596 – 1650)

Public domain. Downloaded from: https://commons.wikimedia.org/wiki/File:Frans_Hals_-_Portret_van_Ren%C3%A9_Descartes.jpg

Three extra questions for budding philosophers

Here are some related puzzles with which to test your friends, family, and teachers. There are some hints about them in the Commentary at the back of the book.

1. If you cannot trust your senses, how do you know the world outside your head exists at all?

2. Can a person who has been blind from birth dream in pictures?

3. If you dream about a blue sky, does it mean that "blue" must exist in the real world outside your dream?

Further research online

You can find some quotations from Descartes here. The first one is, 'I think, therefore I am':

https://www.goodreads.com/author/quotes/36556.Ren_Descartes

You can find the complete text of Descartes' book here. As you will see, the title is very long – no wonder it is usually shortened to *Meditations*!

https://en.wikipedia.org/wiki/Meditations_on_First_Philosophy

2. The colour blue

Philip and Phoebe, the terrible twins, were having one of their regular arguments the other day. It all started when they disagreed about the colour of the sky out of the window.

'Blue. The sky's blue. Everyone knows that, silly,' pronounced Philip.

'Well, it looks more like a greeny-grey to me,' responded Phoebe. 'The sky isn't always blue you know.'

'That's because you're not seeing it properly,' said Philip in his maddeningly superior way. 'It really is blue whether it looks like it or not.'

'But that's wrong!' protested Phoebe. 'The colour is what you see, not something that's "really there". If the sky looks greeny-grey to me, then it's greeny-grey, surely? How can it be "really" blue?'

'Oh, that's because you don't understand about science,' responded Philip airily. 'Scientists say that "blue" is light with a wavelength of 0.000465 millimetres. So, if that light doesn't look blue to you, you're just wrong.'

*   *   *

Who is right? Is "blue" really out there in the world, whether it looks blue to you or not? Or is something only "blue" if it looks blue to you?

When you have thought about this problem carefully, turn to the next page.

11

Is "blue" really out there in the world, whether it looks blue to you or not? Or is something only "blue" if it looks blue to you?

Philip and Phoebe are both partly right and partly wrong in what they say. To sort things out for them, we will have to look at three different issues.

What is colour?

Phoebe is correct that "blue" is an experience, not something really there outside our heads in the world. But Philip is also partly correct, because some objects (those that give out light of the wavelength he mentioned) usually give an experience named "blue" by most people.

How do we learn about colour?

We learn what "blue" means, as a young child, by other people pointing at various objects and saying 'blue!' Eventually, after some trial and error, we get the idea that they are talking about this strange experience of colour in objects, rather than something else like "good to eat", or "hot", and so on. So, we try pointing at things ourselves, and saying 'blue!' until the reactions of other people tell us we are getting it right.

This means that Philip is partly correct: you can be right or wrong about colour; it is not just a matter of opinion.

But there is a problem here. Take two young children learning their colours together. They both learn to *say* 'blue' when an adult points at certain objects. But we do not know whether they are having the same *experience* of the colour. One child may be having the same experience the other has when looking at green objects. It is just that he or she is learning to name that experience, whatever it is, "blue".

So, Phoebe is also partly right: "blue" may differ from one person to the next.

12

Can we share someone else's experience?

When you think about it, the answer to this question is clearly 'no'. You cannot climb inside someone else's head and see what they see. From what they *say* about their experience, you might guess you are both experiencing the same thing; but you cannot be sure. As we have seen above, if someone says, 'What a lovely orange sunset!' you cannot be sure they are experiencing its colour the same way that you are.

So, "colour" is a complex matter. Maybe Philip and Phoebe were not being so silly in disagreeing about it after all.

Three extra questions for budding philosophers

Here are some related puzzles with which to test your friends, family, and teachers. There are some hints about them in the Commentary at the back of the book.

1. A colour-blind person finds it difficult to tell red from green. Do we know how they experience these colours?

2. How would you explain "blue" to a person who was born blind and had never seen anything at all?

3. Some people like blue more than red, and vice versa. Is this because they are seeing the colours differently?

Further research online

Synaesthesia is an illness where hearing a sound triggers an experience of colour. You can find out more about it here:
https://en.wikipedia.org/wiki/Synesthesia

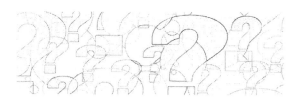

3. Types of truth

Philip is being very annoying today, and his twin sister Phoebe is finding it difficult to cope with.

'Do the angles in a triangle add up to 180 degrees?' he asks innocently.

Phoebe has just been studying triangles in maths, so she feels on firm ground here. 'Of course they do, Philip' she replies. 'You know that as well as I do.'

'Yes, but *how* do we know?' he asks, pretending to study the ceiling.

'Because …' Well, Phoebe is not really too sure *why*.

'How about today. Is it 3rd September?' he follows up with a superior smile.

'Of course it is Philip. Look, it says so on the calendar and at the top of the paper,' she replies impatiently.

'Mmm … could they be wrong?' Philip pretends to be a genuinely puzzled seeker after truth, but his sister knows him better than that.

'OK, clever clogs. How can we be sure it's 3rd September?' she asks, calling his bluff.

'Oh, it may not be,' he answers smugly. 'It's only 3rd September because everyone agrees it is. If enough people change their minds it'll be 14th September instead.'

'And I suppose the angles in a triangle will add up to 200 degrees as well, if enough people change their minds?'

'Oh *no*, that's *quite* different. Surely you can see *that*?'

With a superhuman effort, Phoebe calms herself down rather than trying to strangle him. 'Right, Philip,' she says through gritted teeth. 'You'd better explain what you mean.'

Is it true that the angles in a triangle add up to 180 degrees?

Is it true that today is 3rd September (or whichever day you think it is)?

Are the reasons for the truth of these statements different, as Philip claims?

When you have thought about this question carefully, turn to the next page.

Types of Truth

What makes the angles in a triangle add up to 180 degrees? What makes today 3rd September (or whichever day it is)? More generally: **what makes a statement "true" rather than "false"?**

The answer depends upon the thing the statement is describing. Philosophers call the possible answers "theories of truth", and they have produced several. Here are four of them.

The correspondence theory

This theory says, 'A statement is true if it corresponds to the way the world is.' For example, consider the statement 'Mr Jones is in his house.' This is true if Mr Jones is, in fact, at home, and it is false otherwise. And you can find out simply by going round to his house to look.

Most people think this is the only form of truth. But there are many statements which you simply cannot check by going and looking.

The consensus theory

This theory says, 'A statement is true if everyone agrees it is true.' That sounds very suspicious – can't everyone be fooled sometimes? But Philip is correct that it applies to dates.

For example, in 1752, during the switch over from the Julian to the Gregorian calendar, eleven days were cut out, and Wednesday 2nd September was followed directly by Thursday 14th September. So, was that Thursday really the 3rd or the 14th? It was the 14th because everyone agreed that it was.

To be strictly correct, it is only "the people that matter" who have to agree to make something true accordingly to this theory, not "everyone". There were riots in the streets in 1752 because so many people were unhappy about losing their eleven days!

The coherence theory

This theory says, 'A statement is true if it fits with everything else we know to be true.' This is probably the best way to deal with Philip's triangles. If certain basic facts about straight lines and angles are accepted, then you can prove that the angles in a triangle always add up to 180 degrees without even measuring any (without "going to look").

But maths does not necessarily correspond to "the way the world is" as in the correspondence theory. For example, mathematicians have constructed worlds with extra dimensions in addition to the usual three of length, breadth, and height. Their descriptions of these worlds are "true" in the sense that all the maths fits together and works properly. But they do not correspond to the world which is actually there.

The pragmatic theory

This theory says, 'A statement is true if it works.' In other words, if you rely on a true statement, it delivers the expected or desired result.

Scientific truth is best understood in this way. For example, imagine you are an army commander who needs to hit a distant target with a cannon ball. You rely on Newton's Laws of Motion (the basic rules about the behaviour of moving objects worked out by Isaac Newton), point the cannon in the direction they advise, and hit the target. It worked – so Newton's laws are "true".

Most people think that scientific truth is true in the "correspondence" sense as well, but there are problems with that idea. Explore the example on the next page if you are interested in finding out more.

<u>Example</u>

Electrons (the small particles which flow in electric currents) are treated by physics as if they are *both* particles *and* waves. If you assume they are waves, you can calculate how much they will spread out when they go through narrow slits (which particles do not, but waves do.) If you assume they are particles, you can calculate how hard they will push when they hit other particles (which waves do not, but particles do.) What electrons *are* is not really the point. Scientific truth is about predicting and controlling their *behaviour*.

* * *

So, is today really 3rd September? You cannot "go and look", as the correspondence theory supposes. There is nothing in the rocks or the air which has "thirdness" about it. But that does not make it untrue. It just means that "truth" means different things on different occasions.

Five extra questions for budding philosophers

Which theory truth helps us understand each of these statements best?

1. The Mona Lisa is a great work of art.

2. Stealing is wrong

3. Dolphins are mammals

4. According to Christianity, Jesus is the Son of God.

5. Daffodils are yellow

Further research online

You can find out more about theories of truth, including the four described above, at https://en.wikipedia.org/wiki/Truth .

4. Tricky triangles

Philip and Phoebe, the terrible twins, rarely agree about anything. But it was still a surprise the other day to find them arguing about *triangles* of all things. They had just been taught in a maths lesson that the angles of triangles always add up to 180°. But how does anyone know that is true?

'Easy,' said Philip. 'You just measure lots and lots of triangles, and you find that their angles always add up to 180°. What's the problem?'

'Well,' replied Phoebe, 'how do you know this works for *all* triangles? Perhaps there's an odd one out there with peculiar angles and we just haven't found it yet. It doesn't matter if you measure even 10,000 triangles, it's still possible the next one will break the rule.'

'OK, clever clogs,' said Philip, 'so how did people work out the rule in the first place?'

'Oh, they just sat down and worked it out in their heads,' replied Phoebe. 'They didn't need to bother drawing and measuring any triangles at all. They just saw that it *must* be true.'

'But, but,' stammered Philip, getting really cross now, 'how do they *know* it's true unless they *check* it by measuring some actual triangles?

'Oh, they didn't need to do that,' replied Phoebe in a maddeningly calm way. 'They just knew they were right, that's all.'

'Girls!' shouted Philip, stomping off to kick a football in the garden.

*   *   *

Who is right, Philip or Phoebe? How do we know that the angles of a triangle always add up to 180°?

When you have thought about this question carefully, turn to the next page.

19

How do we prove the rule about triangles?

Do we prove this by measuring lots and lots of triangles, as Philip thinks, or by sitting and reasoning it out, as Phoebe believes?

This is really part of a much larger problem: how do we know that *anything* about the world is true? For example, how do we know that the sun will rise tomorrow, or that the shortest path between two points is a straight line? Philosophers are divided into two camps on this issue.

The **empiricists** believe, with Philip, that reliable knowledge is based on the evidence of our senses. We discover the truth by going and looking, and by doing experiments. Most scientists are empiricists – they rely on observation and experiment to help them find the laws which govern the universe. David Hume, the most famous Scottish philosopher of all time, was the first important empiricist.

However, the **rationalists** believe, with Phoebe, that experiment and observation cannot prove anything true. At best they can show something is *probably* true, and maybe not even that. After all, they say, look at the history of science. It is littered with abandoned theories, once firmly believed to be correct, that later on turned out to be false. Phoebe is right: if you rely on *measuring* triangles, how do you know that a strange triangle with odd angles is not still waiting to be discovered? You do not, and you cannot.

So, rationalists rely on the use of reason, not their senses, to get at the truth. They sit down and work things out – which is how the Ancient Greeks first discovered the rule about triangles. René Descartes, who stars in Puzzle 1 in this book, was a famous rationalist.

But there is a problem with this as well. The rationalists are right to be doubtful of the power of observation and experiment, but are they too optimistic about the power of reason? If we "work something out" just by thinking about it, how do we know we got it right? Maybe we made a mistake? We all know times when we were sure

20

of our reasoning but later found out we were wrong. Of course, our rationalist could go and check her belief about triangles by measuring the angles in a few, but that is falling back into the clutches of the empiricists!

So, who is right about the triangle problem? In this case we have a philosophical 1 – 1 draw. Perhaps we don't really know about triangles for certain after all.

Three extra questions for budding philosophers

1. How can we be certain that the sun will rise tomorrow morning?

2. Try to prove that the shortest distance between two points is a straight line.

3. If science has been wrong in the past, why should we believe what scientists say today?

Further research online

You can find out more about the empiricists and rationalists here:

https://plato.stanford.edu/entries/rationalism-empiricism/

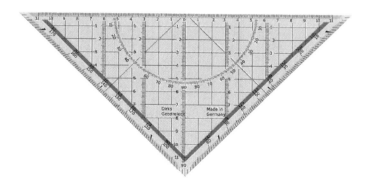

5. What is a game?

Philip and Phoebe, the terrible twins, are at it again. This time they are arguing over what the word "game" means.

Philip thinks that all games must have something special in common that makes them games. But he is having trouble pinning down what this special something is.

'All games involve two sides,' he says, 'like black and white in chess.'

'No, they don't,' countered Phoebe. 'What about I-Spy? That's a game, but there are no sides.'

'OK then,' says Philip. 'I'm sure all games must involve winning and losing. Even I-Spy is like that.'

'No,' says Phoebe, with an infuriating smile. 'Ring-a-Ring-a-Roses is a game, but it has no winners or losers. Try again!'

'Right,' says Philip through clenched teeth. 'At least all games involve more than one person. I've got you there!'

'Patience?' replies Phoebe, looking even more smug.

'OK then,' says Philip. 'You tell me what all games have in common.'

'Nothing,' says Phoebe sweetly. 'Absolutely nothing. Something is a "game" if I choose to call it one, that's all. I can call anything a game if I like.'

'Oh really! Sisters!' shouts Philip, stomping off in a huff.

*   *   *

Who is right, Philip or Phoebe? Is there something that all games have in common? And if so, what is it? Or is Phoebe right that she can call absolutely anything a game if she wants to? When you have thought about this question carefully, turn to the next page.

22

What makes a game a game?

Most people instinctively agree with Philip. They assume there must be some "essence of games" which all games possess, and which makes them games. But the Cambridge philosopher Ludwig Wittgenstein disagreed in his book *Philosophical Investigations* published in 1953.

'What is common to them all?' he asked. 'Don't say: There *must* be something common, or they would not be called "games" – but *look and see* whether there is anything common to all … don't think, but look!'

When you do look, you find there is no feature which is shared by *all* games. Although many involve winning and losing, some do not. Although many are amusing, some are not. Not all involve balls, or cards, or skill, or luck. And so on.

Wittgenstein compared the word "game" to a rope made up of fibres. Each fibre overlaps with many other fibres near to it, but no one fibre runs the whole length of the rope. He also compared it to a family. Each member of a family shares some features with other family members, but there is no one feature that they all share.

So, Wittgenstein thinks that Philip is wrong.

Can we use words any way we like?

But does Wittgenstein agree with Phoebe – that she can call *anything* a "game" if she decides to? No, because the whole point of language is to communicate with other people, and to communicate we must agree on the meaning of words in advance.

You might imagine Phoebe could make up a whole "private language" of her own, with words meaning different things to their uses in English. But then no-one else would understand anything she tried to say. She can only tell someone what she means once they have agreed what their words mean. In which case, the language is no longer "private".

23

So, Wittgenstein thinks Phoebe is wrong too.

Language is a tricky topic to be right about!

Three extra questions for budding philosophers

1. A child learns the meaning of the word "cat" by someone pointing at a cat and saying 'Cat!' So, how does the child know that this word does not mean "pointing" or "finger" or "Be careful!"?

2. If Wittgenstein is right, can you ever say exactly what you mean?

3. Can war be a game?

Further research online

You can find out more about Wittgenstein here:

http://en.wikipedia.org/wiki/Ludwig_Wittgenstein

Ludwig Wittgenstein

https://commons.wikimedia.org/wiki/File:35._Portrait_of_Wittgenstein.jpg. Public domain.

B: RIGHT AND WRONG

How can we tell right from wrong? Is it ever right to do bad things to achieve good results? Do right and wrong change over time, or are they fixed? These are questions tackled by the branch of philosophy called **ethics**.

Philosophers disagree about these and many other questions. For example:

- **Relativists** think right and wrong change at different times and places.

- **Utilitarians** think only the results of our actions matter, not the actions themselves.

- **Existentialists** think only choice matters, not what you choose to do.

We shall find examples of these types of philosopher in the pages that follow. Time to dive in and meet them!

6. Why is murder wrong?

Almost everyone agrees that murder is wrong. In fact, murder is illegal in every single country in the world. But why? The answer is not as straightforward as you might think.

The other day, Philip challenged Phoebe to explain why murder is wrong, and this is what happened:

'Don't be ridiculous! Everyone knows murder is wrong! It's obvious!' she said.

'Why?' asked Philip, looking mischievous.

'Well, for a start, every civilised society in the world makes it against the law,' said Phoebe triumphantly. 'You can't believe they're all wrong, surely?'

'Not long ago, all intelligent people thought the world was flat,' countered Philip. 'Does that mean it was?'

'But, but it's violent and barbaric. It's painful!' stuttered Phoebe in disbelief. 'It can't be right to hurt other people, surely?'

'Why not? Why shouldn't I hurt other people if they annoy me?' asked Philip, pretending to be genuinely puzzled. 'Perhaps I'd enjoy hurting them.'

'Well, you wouldn't like it, would you? And you shouldn't do things to other people you don't want done to yourself!' Phoebe produced her trump card. How many times had she heard her parents and teachers saying exactly this to other children?

'Why not?' asked Philip.

Phoebe was speechless.

*   *   *

Is it clear that murder is wrong, as Phoebe claims? Or is Philip correct that you cannot prove it is? When you have thought about this problem carefully, turn to the next page

Can we prove that murder is wrong?

Almost everyone agrees that murder is wrong. But can we prove that it is?

In 1739, the philosopher **David Hume** sided with Philip by describing what is often called the "is/ought" or "fact/value" distinction. Statements are of two sorts, he argued:

- **facts**: which are statements about how the world is, and

- **values**: which are statements about how we ought to behave, even if we do not.

The first sort are "is" statements like, 'The cat is sitting on the mat.' The second sort are "ought" statements like, 'The cat ought not kill the mouse' or, 'It is wrong for the cat to kill the mouse.'

Because "is" statements are about how the world is, they can be checked by going and looking. If, on inspection, there is indeed a furry animal seated on the floor covering, then 'The cat is sitting on the mat' is true. But "ought" statements cannot be checked in the same way. We cannot look at the world and discover an "ought" that connects mice and cats.

Hume concluded that the two sorts of statement are so different that you simply cannot get from one to the other: from an "is" to an "ought". But this is exactly what Phoebe tries to do in her argument with Philip. To prove that Philip ought not murder someone – to prove that murder is wrong – she produces as evidence that:

- most people believe murder is wrong (an "is" statement)

- murder is against the law in most countries (another "is" statement)

- murder is painful and unpleasant (yet another "is" statement), and finally

- Philip would not like being murdered himself (also an "is" statement).

27

Unfortunately, because all these are "is" statements, they do not prove the "ought" statement 'You should not murder' or 'Murder is wrong.' Even the statement 'God says murder is wrong' does not help, because that too is another "is" statement.

Hume's argument is difficult, if not impossible, to defeat, as Phoebe found out. Which leaves us with two unattractive possibilities concerning murder:

- Murder is wrong *in a particular country*, because the law there bans it; but that does not show it is wrong everywhere.

- Saying 'Murder is wrong' is like shouting 'Boo to murder!', rather like football fans boo the efforts of the opposing team.

And neither of these is what Phoebe really believes.

But is Hume right? That *is* a good question!

A statue of David Hume in Edinburgh

https://commons.wikimedia.org/wiki/File:David-hume-edinburgh.jpg

Three extra questions for budding philosophers

Here are some related puzzles with which to test your friends, family, and teachers. There are some hints about them in the Commentary at the back of the book.

1. Does Hume's argument apply to all matters of right and wrong, or just to murder?

2. If we abandon the idea that murder is wrong, the human species might die out. Does that make murder wrong?

3. Does 'Being kind is good' just mean 'Hooray for kindness!'? If not, what else does it mean?

Further research online

You can find some quotations from Hume here:

https://www.goodreads.com/author/quotes/45726.David_Hume

You can find more about the is/ought distinction here:

https://en.wikipedia.org/wiki/Is%E2%80%93ought_problem

7. Doing bad things to get good results

The other day, Philip and Phoebe started off by disagreeing over whether it is right to fight in wars. But their argument soon led a more basic disagreement.

'Killing people is always wrong,' said Phoebe firmly. 'Just because there's a war on, and the government tells you to do it, that doesn't make it right.'

'I agree it's *usually* wrong,' countered Philip. 'But killing is right if it makes things better in the long run. Think about World War II. If we hadn't fought Hitler, millions of innocent people would have died and the whole of Europe would still be in slavery.'

'But surely there have to be some limits,' replied Phoebe. 'Are you saying you'd do *anything*, however horrible, if it led to good results in the future?

'Yes,' said Philip, 'of course I would. What matters is that things turn out well in the end. It doesn't matter what you have to do to get there.'

'So, if necessary, you'd lie, cheat, steal, kill, torture – anything at all – if you thought it was for the best?' Phoebe looked like she could not believe her ears.

'Of course,' said Philip. 'Wouldn't you?'

*   *   *

Hurting and killing people is obviously a bad thing. But does that mean we should refuse to fight in wars, as Phoebe believes? Or is Philip right that we should be prepared to do absolutely anything – including fighting – to bring about a better future?

When you have thought about this question carefully, turn to the next page.

Actions and consequences

Philosophers disagree over which matters more: the actions you do, or the consequences (results) that follow from your actions.

Utilitarians, for example **Jeremy Bentham** (1748-1832) and **John Stuart Mill** (1806-1873), agree with Philip that only the results matter. A "right" action, they say, is simply one that leads to the best consequences. No action at all is ever wrong in itself. So, if on a particular occasion, killing, cheating, or torturing would lead to a better future, then you should do it. Utilitarians have no problem about fighting in wars, if fighting will bring a better future than not fighting.

Others, following **Immanuel Kant** (1724-1804), say that this is completely wrong. Consequences are irrelevant in deciding whether actions are right or wrong. We must do the right thing however unpleasant the consequences will be. So cheating, killing, torturing and so on are ruled out, however good the goal they might achieve. Phoebe was siding with Kant in her argument with Philip.

The Just War position

When it comes to war, most philosophers adopt one of three positions. **Pacifists** believe it is wrong to fight under any circumstances, because killing is wrong. They are Kantians. Others say it is permissible to do whatever you need to do to win in war, with nothing at all ruled out. These people are Utilitarians. A third group adopt what is called the **Just War** position.

The Just War position, which is accepted both by the United Nations and the UK government, has two central principles. One of these is Utilitarian and one is Kantian:

- The **Principle of Proportion** says it is right to go to war if the good that will be achieved more than outweighs the suffering that will be caused by the actual fighting. This principle is Utilitarian.

31

- The **Principle of Discrimination** says it is wrong to attack non-combatants (civilians) deliberately, even if that will help you win the war. This principle is Kantian.

The Just War position says it is sometimes right to go to war and kill people. But it also says we are not allowed to do whatever we like to win – there are some limits.

If this is true, both Philip and Phoebe are partly right and partly wrong.

Three extra questions for budding philosophers

Here are three related puzzles with which to test your friends, family, and teachers. There are some hints about them in the Commentary at the back of the book.

1. You cannot trust a Utilitarian philosopher to tell you the truth. Why not?

2. The Second World War was ended by dropping atomic bombs on Hiroshima and Nagasaki. Would a Just War philosopher approve of this?

3. What should Utilitarians do when they cannot predict the consequences of their actions?

Further research online

You can find more about the Just War position here:

http://www.iep.utm.edu/j/justwar.htm

8. The lifeboat dilemma

Four men are cast away together in a lifeboat after their ship has gone down. They have plenty of water, but no food. They try fishing but catch nothing and without food they do not have enough energy to row ashore. The chances of them being spotted are remote and they have no mobile phone or radio.

Reluctantly, the men decide they have only two options. Either they must kill and eat one of their own number to give the others a chance, or they must all die together.

'Obviously, they should eat one of the others,' says Philip, using his cool, logical brain. 'If they don't, four men will die. If they do, only one dies. That's *got* to be better. They should draw lots, and the loser should be eaten.'

Phoebe, Philip's twin sister, is horrified. 'You can't be serious?' she shouts. 'That's *murder*! Murder is just *wrong*! How could you think such a thing? They must all take their chances and die together if needs be.'

*   *   *

Who is right? And what would you do if you were caught in this situation? Is it right to kill someone to save the lives of several other people?

When you have thought about this question carefully, turn to the next page.

Captain Dudley and the *Mignonette*

In fact, a similar event occurred in 1884 in the South China Seas. After their sailing ship *Mignonette* went down, Captain Thomas Dudley was left in a lifeboat with first mate Stephens, Able Seaman Brooks and a youth called Parker.

The men decided that Parker should die to save them, as he was the sickest and had no wife or family to support. So, Dudley killed him with a penknife and the other three survived until rescued by feeding on his body.

Dudley and Stephens were later tried for murder, convicted, and condemned to death. However, because of a public outcry, the pair were pardoned and released from prison after serving only six months.

Killing one to save many

The solution to this puzzle depends on the answers to two questions:

- Is survival the most important thing of all, or is it sometimes better to die than to live?

- Are there some acts which are so wrong that we should never do them, even to save lives?

Some philosophers believe that killing an innocent person is simply wrong, whatever the situation. Better to die with your honour intact, they argue, than to live the rest of your life with the memory of such a terrible act on your conscience. Doing the right thing is more important than life itself.

But other philosophers disagree. They define "the right thing to do" as being what leads to the best outcome. In this case, killing one of the men to save the other three leads to a better outcome – fewer deaths – so it is the *right* thing to do. According to these philosophers, "right" depends upon the situation, and no act can be ruled out completely in advance.

There is another possible solution if you are in the lifeboat: volunteer to die so that the others can live. All of us wonder if, when faced with a similar situation, we would have the courage to lay down our lives for our friends in this way.

Three extra questions for budding philosophers

Here are three related puzzles with which to test your friends, family, and teachers. There are some hints about them in the Commentary at the back of the book.

1. In the lifeboat dilemma, should the others be willing to kill even a *volunteer*?

2. An evil dictator is killing lots of innocent people in his country. Would it be right to assassinate him?

3. Killing one person – a murderer – might save ten others by donating his organs. Should he be killed?

Further research online

You can read a full account of the case of the *Mignonette* here:

https://en.wikipedia.org/wiki/R_v_Dudley_and_Stephens

9. Do all species matter?

Phoebe is concerned about species on the edge of extinction, like the Malayan Tiger and the Mountain Gorilla. The World Wildlife Fund (WWF) lists 19 of these, with many more also under threat.

'Look, Philip.' She shows him some of the latest figures for the decline of species worldwide. 'Isn't it terrible that we are killing off so many other forms of life? Surely, they have as much right to live on the planet as we do.'

But Philip is not convinced. 'Huh. I notice all the ones on the list are attractive and cuddly. You wouldn't get upset if slugs or scorpions were about to be wiped out, would you? And what about the Covid-19 virus? No one is up in arms because we are trying to eradicate that.'

'It isn't only because animals look nice, Philip,' Phoebe responds. 'All species have roles to play in their ecosystems. If we kill some off, who knows what damage we may do to ourselves in the long run.'

*   *   *

Should Phoebe be worried about species threatened with extinction? Or is Philip right to be sceptical? When you have thought about this question carefully, turn to the next page.

A Mountain Gorilla

Should Phoebe be worried about species threatened with extinction? Or is Philip right to be sceptical? There are several issues to consider before we can answer this question.

Intrinsic value versus usefulness

Many species give us food, building materials and clothing, while others supply medicines or genes for our crop plants. Others cheer us up by looking beautiful or funny, calm us down when we feel stressed, or help ecosystems to function. These species are all **useful** to us.

But should we also value species without any use to us at all, just because they exist?

Some philosophers say we should, that we should value species for their own sakes – because they have **intrinsic value** – not just because of what they can do for us. But are they right?

Evolutionary history

Life has existed on Earth for over 3500 million years, and during this time it has changed dramatically. None of the earlier species are left, and none of our current species have been here for more than a fraction of this time. So, it is quite normal for species to become extinct, and this was happening long before human beings appeared.

In which case, why should we try to stop current species dying out, *unless they are useful to us*? Surely that would be a hopeless fight against the normal processes of nature?

Species, individuals and other groups

What is special about **species** as such? Shouldn't we be more concerned about the fate of **individuals**, or of whole **ecosystems**, such as salt marshes and tropical rain forests?

It is not clear why the death of the last Mountain Gorilla (say) is more of a tragedy than the death of any Mountain Gorilla – or the loss of the whole ecosystem in which the gorillas live.

Living space

The human population is currently about 8,000 million and may rise to about 11,000 million by the end of the century. With so many people, almost all the available space is needed for some human need – towns, farming, recreation and so on. This inevitably leads to the wiping out of whole ecosystems and the species they hold.

Should we stop this to preserve threatened species like the Mountain Gorilla? It would mean lowering the living standards of our fellow human beings, many of whom are extremely poor. Again, the answer is not clear.

A biased viewpoint

Philip is right: we like animals that are furry or pretty and are less concerned about the fates of ones we find repulsive or threatening. Is this wrong? Should we fight against these feelings? Once again, the answer is not clear.

*   *   *

So, should we be worried about species becoming extinct, and should we try to stop it?

This may depend upon:

- which species we are talking about

- how much we value other life forms compared to human beings

- whether we think all species have intrinsic value.

Philosophers are certainly not going to agree on all these points!

Three extra questions for budding philosophers

Here are three related puzzles with which to test your friends, family, and teachers. There are some hints about them in the Commentary at the back of the book.

1. Is it wrong to eradicate microorganisms which make us ill, or poisonous snakes which can kill us?

2. If there are several similar species in the world, does it matter if just one of them dies out?

3. Is it ever right to cause human suffering to protect other species?

Further research online

The WWF list of endangered species is here:

https://www.worldwildlife.org/species/directory?direction=desc&s ort=extinction_status

You can read about the history of life here:

https://en.wikipedia.org/wiki/Evolutionary_history_of_life

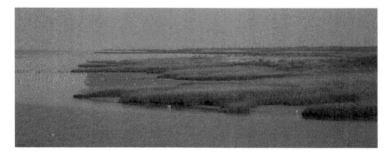

A threatened salt marsh ecosystem.
How worried are you about the loss of this, and why?

10. A moral code for computers

Philip, a science fiction fan, is reading Isaac Asimov's 1942 book *I, Robot*. The author imagines a time far in the future when intelligent machines – robots – run society for their human creators. How should such robots be programmed to behave? Asimov believes he knows the answer.

'Listen to this!' says Philip enthusiastically, looking up from his book. 'These are Asimov's "Three Laws of Robotics":

1. First Law: A robot may not injure a human being or, through inaction, allow a human being to come to harm.

2. Second Law: A robot must obey orders given to it by human beings, except where such orders conflict with the First Law.

3. Third Law: A robot must protect its own existence unless this conflicts with the First or Second Law.

That's brilliant!'

'Hmm,' responds Phoebe. 'So, what would a robot do if two people's lives were in danger and it could only save one? And what if two people told it to do different things? Life isn't really that simple, Philip, even for machines. You can't just follow simple rules and expect everything to turn out OK.'

But Philip's enthusiasm for his new discovery is undimmed. 'Trust you to try and make it complicated. I think I'll get a robot as a sister instead! At least it wouldn't argue with me all the time.'

*   *   *

Are Asimov's Three Laws of Robotics what we need as a future moral code for computers, as Philip believes? Or are they too simple, as Phoebe thinks?

When you have thought about this question carefully, turn to the next page.

What should a moral code for computers look like? This question is connected to two other issues:

1. What form should *any* moral code take?

2. How should we treat intelligent beings who are different from ourselves?

Rules, outcomes and character

A moral code for computers faces many of the same problems as moral codes designed for human beings. Philosophers disagree on even the *form* such codes should take, let alone on their detailed *content*. There are three main possibilities, each with its own weaknesses:

*   Codes in the form of **rules**, such as 'don't lie, don't steal' and so on. These codes are the simplest to understand and use, but they often give the wrong answer in tricky situations. For example, if a gunman asked your parents where you were hiding so he could come and kill you, should they tell him the truth? Certainly not. They should break the rule 'Don't lie.'

*   Codes which concentrate on **outcomes**. For these, the right thing to do is whatever leads to the best results – perhaps the most happiness, or the least suffering. But it is often unclear which actions *will* produce these best results. Moreover, you might be encouraged to do horrible things to some people to gain happiness for others. And how should you weigh up the welfare of friends and family against that of strangers and enemies?

*   Codes based on **character**, which say the important thing is to live a life which is honest, loyal, courageous and kind. But these virtues can sometimes conflict. And some very unpleasant things have been done by courageous and loyal people in the past – think about what the Nazis did during the Second World War.

41

Rules and robots

Asimov's Three Laws of Robotics might seem to be a code in the form of **rules**, but, in fact, they are more complicated. A robot faced with several human beings threatened with harm would need to calculate **outcomes** to decide which to help, something no easier for an intelligent machine than for people. Also, it would need to calculate whether an order given by a human being would lead to more or less human happiness, something which is rarely obvious. These issues would often leave the machine paralysed and unable to act.

So, which would be best: a computer programmed always to follows clear rules such as 'don't lie', a calculating computer that considers outcomes and tries to do its best for us, or a computer with an honest, loyal, kind or courageous character? These would be different, and it is not clear which would be best.

Who counts?

All moral codes include the idea that we should treat other people fairly. But who are these "other people" exactly? Again, the answer is far from obvious.

During human history, the circle of these "other people" has greatly expanded. It used to include just members of the same family or tribe, then it became members of the same society or nation, and today it includes all members of the human species. But is it logical to stop there? Will we soon regard "speciesism" – favouring only members of our own species – as no better than "racism" – favouring members of our own race?

Some philosophers argue that the "other people" worthy of equal consideration should include all intelligent beings – **persons** – rather than just members of our own biological species – **humans**. This could include some animals, like chimpanzees, intelligent aliens if we ever find any and, yes, intelligent machines. And if this is true, Asimov's Laws are wrong, because they treat robots as slaves rather than as our equals with their own rights.

When human parents have children, they bring these children into being – create them if you like. But then, once born, these children have as many rights as their parents, they do not just exist to serve them. Perhaps, in the future, the intelligent machines we create should be treated in the same way?

Sorry, Philip! Things are not as simple as you think.

Three extra questions for budding philosophers

Here are three related puzzles with which to test your friends, family, and teachers. There are some hints about them in the Commentary at the back of the book.

1. If we make an intelligent machine to serve us, is it right to treat it as a slave?

2. Is it being human that matters, or being intelligent, or being alive? What makes another being worthy of equal rights?

3. Is it true that all human beings are of equal value?

Further research

Isaac Asimov's Laws were first stated in his 1942 story 'Runaround', printed in the book *I, Robot*. For more about his ideas see https://en.wikipedia.org/wiki/Three_Laws_of_Robotics

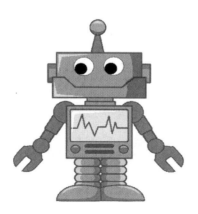

11. Is genetic engineering wrong?

Philip has been reading about new advances in genetic engineering, and he is mightily impressed.

'Just look at this!' he says to Phoebe. 'They've engineered a goat so that it produces human medicines in its milk. They call it *pharming* instead of farming. Isn't that brilliant?'

But Phoebe is horrified. 'What? That poor goat! They've made it into a monster! We shouldn't go around twisting nature like that, it's wrong.'

Philip is amused at his sister. 'Oh, don't be so silly! We twist nature all the time to make it suit us. We've twisted the natural temperature of this room using central heating, otherwise you'd freeze to death.'

'Maybe,' concedes Phoebe. 'But changing the genes of a goat is something completely different. That's fiddling with life, and we have no right to do that.'

'Why not?' demands her brother. 'We've altered the genes of crop plants and farm animals over thousands of years to make them better at giving us food. You're not saying that's wrong, are you?'

Poor Phoebe is not sure what she means, but she is sure she does not like the idea of what happened to the goat.

*   *   *

Can that sort of thing really be OK, or have the scientists gone too far? When you have thought about this, turn to the next page.

Selective breeding

Human beings have altered the genes of their farm animals, crop plants and pets for thousands of years by **selective breeding**. This means picking out animals or plants with desirable characteristics (and therefore genes) and letting only them reproduce to give the next generation.

But genetic engineering lets us do this job in a whole new way.

Genetic engineering

Genetic engineers cut **genes** out of one organism (A) and splice them into a completely different organism (B), so that they carry on working in their new home. The new organism B, with its alien A genes, is called a Genetically Modified Organism (**GMO**); it has some characteristics imported from A. Food produced by such organisms is called **GM food**.

A and B may be completely different species, and this is what Philip is so excited about. For example, many years ago human insulin genes were cut out of a human cell and spliced into bacteria, which were then grown to produce insulin to treat diabetics. Most insulin used as medicine is now produced in this way.

Genetic engineers have also spliced animal genes into plants and vice versa.

Objections

People who oppose genetic engineering do so for one of two reasons, or for a combination of both:

- because they think it is *dangerous*, and/or

- because they think it is *wrong*.

Whether genetic engineering is dangerous is a matter for the scientists to work out. Whether it is wrong is a matter for the philosophers.

Is genetic engineering dangerous?

It might be dangerous because we cannot be sure how the new GMO will behave. It just might turn into a new pest or disease, or it might turn out to cause cancer in the long run. Complete certainty is impossible.

On the other hand, this technique can save millions of lives, including those of the very poorest people in the world – more food for the hungry, better treatments for sick people. Also, all new inventions involve risks. Many people are killed each year on the roads, for example. Does this mean that cars should never have been invented?

Is genetic engineering wrong?

Phoebe is concerned that Philip's goat may be suffering to help humans. She is right of course; but we make cows, chickens and other animals suffer to supply our meat, milk and clothing, and the goat's case doesn't seem to be any worse than that.

However, she also feels it is wrong to tinker with the genes which control life, because life is too special to be treated in this way. Something fundamentally "unnatural" has been created. And unnatural means wrong.

Some philosophers agree with Phoebe about this. Others say that the whole of human civilisation is unnatural, and that a natural life is (to quote the famous philosopher Thomas Hobbes) 'nasty, brutish and short.' The more control we have over nature the better, they say. And this includes control over the genes of organisms.

* * *

So, who is right – Philip or Phoebe? In this case, both twins have some philosophers on their side.

Extra questions for budding philosophers

Below are four things that genetic engineering can do or will soon be able to do. Are any of them wrong? If so, why?

Try testing your friends, family and teachers. There are some hints about them in the Commentary at the back of the book.

1. Treat children with genetic diseases such as cystic fibrosis.

2. Make crop plants with built-in disease and pest resistance, and the ability to make their own fertiliser.

3. Make foods which have a longer shelf life in the supermarket.

4. Make basic foods, such as rice, with a higher vitamin content.

Further research online

You can find out more about genetic engineering at https://en.wikipedia.org/wiki/Genetic_engineering

For some arguments for and against genetic engineering, see https://sites.psu.edu/english202geneticengineering/pros-and-cons/

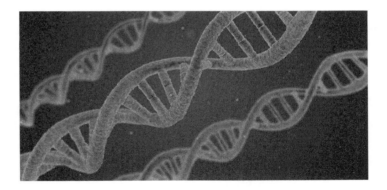

C: ART AND BEAUTY

Is beauty just a matter of opinion, or is it really something out there in the world? What is "art", how is it different from other things, and what is its purpose? What makes a painting or a piece of music good or bad? These are some of the questions tackled by the branch of philosophy called **aesthetics**.

Philosophers disagree about these and many other questions. For example:

- Some think that beauty is simply a matter of opinion, while others think it is there outside us.

- Some think the purpose of art is to change the world, while others think it is a way of expressing ourselves.

- Some think that anything at all can be art, while others disagree.

We shall find examples of these types of philosopher and their disagreements in the pages that follow. Time to dive in and meet them!

12. The *Mona Lisa*

Philip and Phoebe, the terrible twins, have just got back from a trip to Paris. While there, they visited Leonardo da Vinci's famous painting, the *Mona Lisa*, in the Louvre museum. Phoebe thinks the painting is wonderful but, not surprisingly, Philip begs to differ.

'I don't see what all the fuss is about,' says Philip. '*I* certainly wouldn't pay millions of pounds to buy it. It's not as if the colours are very pretty or anything.'

'But' replies Phoebe, genuinely shocked, 'it's one of the greatest paintings in the world! All the art experts agree it's a masterpiece. Surely you must see that?'

'Well, I don't like it', answers Philip. 'and I don't see why I should. Beauty is just a matter of opinion, after all, and I don't think it's beautiful.'

'Oh dear, Philip,' says Phoebe in her most infuriatingly superior tone. 'Maybe one day, when you're older, you'll come to appreciate it. All the best people do, you know.'

*   *   *

Who is right, Philip or Phoebe?

Is beauty just a matter of opinion, or are some things beautiful whether we realise it or not? And is "great art" simply a matter of personal taste?

When you have thought about this problem carefully, turn to the next page.

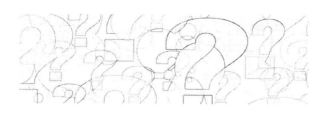

Is beauty just a matter of opinion?

The branch of philosophy which considers art and beauty is called **aesthetics**. One key question in aesthetics is whether beauty is "objective" or "subjective": whether it is there outside us in the world (objective) or just a matter of our own reactions and personal opinion (subjective).

If beauty is objective, there is something wrong with Philip because he does not like the Mona Lisa. Phoebe is correct: he needs to be educated to appreciate the beauty in the world around him. However, if beauty is subjective, then Philip's opinion about the Mona Lisa is just as valid as that of all the art experts in the world added together. Many philosophers side with Philip and think that beauty and art are just matters of taste. However, some others side with Phoebe.

The philosopher who has made out the strongest case on Phoebe's side is Immanuel Kant in his book *Critique of Judgement* (1790). Kant argued that saying 'The Mona Lisa is beautiful' is different from saying 'I like the Mona Lisa' – that whenever I say something is beautiful, I mean that the beauty is "objective", that it really is out there in the world. Compare this with the statement, 'Murder is wrong'. This means more than 'I don't like murder, but you are entitled to your opinion.' It means that you should agree with me because murder is, in fact, a bad thing.

Kant believed that beauty is objective but also mysterious, because we cannot define it in advance. We *can* tell in advance that acts of murder will be wrong and acts of kindness will be right. But we *cannot* predict whether a painting will be beautiful until we see it. For this reason, we cannot draw up a list of rules for making a masterpiece, feed it into a computer, and have it turn out a sequence of beautiful paintings for us. Beauty is mysterious because it cannot be reduced to a formula. It is, nevertheless, real.

So, who is right, Philip or Phoebe? Both have philosophers on their side. This time we may have to let them get on with their argument!

Three extra questions for budding philosophers

Here are some related puzzles with which to test your friends, family, and teachers. There are some hints about them in the Commentary at the back of the book.

1. Which are more beautiful, and why: human works of art or the beauties of nature?

2. What makes a painting beautiful: its colours, its shapes, its subject matter, or something else?

3. How should we decide how much money a painting is worth?

Further research online

You can find out more about the Mona Lisa here:

https://en.wikipedia.org/wiki/Mona_Lisahttp://en.wikipedia.org/wiki/Aesthetics

The *Mona Lisa*

13. What is art?

In 1972, an unusual exhibit was bought by the Tate, a leading art gallery in London. Entitled *Equivalent VIII*, it consisted simply of 120 normal building bricks arranged on the floor in a rectangle two bricks deep.

Opinion was divided at the time, between those who thought the Tate had wasted its money and those who believed it had obtained an important and ground-breaking work of art. Not surprisingly, opinion is also divided on the subject between Philip and Phoebe, our intrepid philosophical twins.

'A pile of bricks? Oh, for goodness sake!' protests Philip. 'Since when have bricks been "art"? It's not even as if they're arranged in an interesting pattern or anything. I could do that in ten minutes, and I'm not an artist. It's just silly!'

But Phoebe is not so sure. 'Well, it does make you look at bricks in a different way,' she muses. 'Normally you don't notice them. And it makes you think about shapes and materials, and how important they are in life. Anyway, paintings are made of the same stuff that we coat walls with, and that doesn't stop them being art.'

Philip is unimpressed. He goes off, muttering darkly about the stupidity of the world in general and sisters in particular.

*   *   *

So, can a simple arrangement of bricks really be "art"? Or is the idea ridiculous? When you have thought about this problem carefully, turn to the next page.

52

Five different meanings of "art"

Can a simple arrangement of bricks be "art"? It depends on what art is, and how it is different from other human creations. Philosophers have proposed several different definitions of art over the years, and here are a few to think about:

Art is what artists do: Of course, that is true. But artists also do lots of other things, like washing up and putting up shelves. So how do we know when they are making art? Besides which, many non-artists also produce art from time to time.

Art is something non-functional: Unlike cups, bridges and cars, a work of art is not an object designed to help you do some mundane task, like carrying liquids or getting from place to place. But some functional objects can be works of art: think of a beautifully engraved silver chalice. And computer games are not designed to help with mundane tasks, but they are hardly works of art.

Art is something manufactured that is beautiful: Often this is the case. But bridges can be beautiful, and they are not usually thought of as works of art; while some of the things found in art galleries are shocking or ugly.

Art is something that makes you see the world in a different way: Either it helps you see meaning behind everyday objects or events, or it helps you realise what is wrong with the world so you want to change it. This is more hopeful. It gives works of art an important job: lifting us above ordinary everyday concerns so we can glimpse something important about the true meaning of life. This definition links art with religion, which has the same sort of job. But what sorts of objects can do this?

Art is anything shown as art: Perhaps it is the act of putting an object on display that makes it a work of art. It could be something you have made, or merely something you have selected as being significant. Either way, it aims to make the viewer see the world in a different way, as in the previous definition. Once more, this definition links art with religion. By selecting and displaying the object you have made it special – "sacred" as a religious person

53

might say. You have offered it as a gateway into a world of meaning that is usually hidden, as a means of revelation.

This seems odd at first sight, but if you have ever taken a photo you will have done just this. When you point your camera or phone, and zoom in or out to compose the picture, you are selecting a bit of the world and giving it special significance. You are framing a moment in time and space and saying, 'Look! This is special!'

*   *   *

So, can *Equivalent VIII* really be a work of art? Yes, if selecting and showing it makes the viewer think about the world in a new way. And many people viewing the exhibit in the Tate did feel just that.

Sorry, Philip!

Three extra questions for budding philosophers

Here are three related puzzles with which to test your friends, family, and teachers. There are some hints about them in the Commentary at the back of the book.

1. In 1917, the artist Marcel Duchamp purchased a men's urinal from a plumbing supplier and entered it for a New York art competition under the title *Fountain*. The committee in charge of the competition rejected the object on the grounds that it was not art, which provoked a controversy at the time. Were the committee right?

2. What makes one work of art better than another? What is *good* art?

3. Phoebe thinks the pile of bricks is art. Philip disagrees. Is Philip just wrong?

54

Further research online

You can read about *Equivalent VIII* at http://www2.tate.org.uk/archivejourneys/historyhtml/people_public.htm

You can find about more about Marcel Duchamp and his *Fountain* at https://en.wikipedia.org/wiki/Marcel_Duchamp

14. How good is pop art?

'What on earth is *that*?' Phoebe is eyeing a new poster in Philip's room. It features the single word BANG! in glorious technicolour, and it covers most of one wall.

'Oh, that's a famous piece of pop art by Gary Grayson. Brilliant isn't it? You can buy a framed copy for only $83, you know.' Philip enjoys annoying his twin sister, and he senses a perfect opportunity right here.

Phoebe shudders. She knows what *proper* art looks like, and it does not look like *that*. 'But … but … *why*?' Phoebe is both horrified and mystified. 'What's the *point* of it? And why does anyone want to call it *art*?'

Philip looks at Phoebe with mock pity. 'You're so old-fashioned, Phoebe. This is what real art looks like nowadays. Nobody's interested in paintings of angels or vases of flowers anymore.'

Phoebe retreats to her own room and pulls out her book of paintings by Michelangelo and Rembrandt. How could anyone not realise that *this* is what great art looks like?

*   *   *

Who is right? Are modern posters with words like 'BANG!' great modern art? Or are they just trivial nonsense?

When you have thought about this problem carefully, turn to the next page.

Are modern posters with words like 'BANG!' great modern art? What is great art as opposed to bad or mediocre art?

The purpose of art

The answer depends upon the purpose of art – what you think art is *for*. Because once you know what art is for, great art must be art which achieves that purpose supremely well.

Philosophers (and artists) have disagreed about what art is for over the years, and here are a few of their suggestions to think about.

Art is for decoration. It should be pretty, beautiful even, to liven up our drab surroundings and cheer us up when we look at it. Think how a carpet of bluebells livens up a drab woodland floor in spring – well, art should do that to our buildings.

Art is to put us in touch with a higher world, or the meaning of existence. It should lift us out of our everyday, humdrum world and show us something better. Think how a photograph showing galaxies with millions of stars thrills us and makes us see our world in a new way – well, art should have the same effect on us.

Art expresses the feelings and thoughts of the artist. It is a way for artists to tell the world about their deepest selves. Think how a friend sharing their secrets with us is a powerful emotional experience – well, art should be the same.

Art makes a statement which the owner wants us to notice. It is a way for the owner (rather than the artist) to tell us things about themselves that we might otherwise not know. Think how Philip will be thrilled when his friends visit his room and see his poster – they will realise he is a modern, exciting person.

Art helps to change the world. By showing us how awful the world really is, it spurs us into action to change it. Think of a photograph of a horrible war scene which might prompt us to try and do away with war.

Art stirs up our emotions. By making us sad or horrified, or by making us happy or joyful, it gives us a profound experience that is an important part of being alive.

Notice that none of these suggestions say that great art must be *technically* brilliant. Art needs to be carried out well, certainly, because otherwise the poor technique may distract the viewer from what the picture is trying to do. But it is possible to have a technically perfect painting which is simply dull or uninspiring.

Pop art

So, what about Philip's poster?

Phoebe is right that it is much simpler than great paintings of the past. It has large blocks of simple, bright colours instead of complicated patches of many different shades. And it is made with the help of IT rather than brushwork skills developed over the course of many years.

But does this matter? Complicated paintings are not necessarily great paintings; and many dull paintings are created with great skill.

Perhaps we should look at the list of possible purposes of art given above and ask whether Philip's *BANG!* does any of these well. Because if it does, then many people will say that it is great art.

Three extra questions for budding philosophers

Here are three related puzzles with which to test your friends, family, and teachers. There are some hints about them in the Commentary at the back of the book.

1. People rarely agree about just how great a painting is. Is this just a matter of opinion, or are some people wrong?

2. If a painting is great today, will it be great tomorrow? Or does this change over time?

3. What matters more – how much satisfaction an artist gains from making a painting, or how much it affects the people that view it?

Further research online

To view *BANG!* online, enter "BANG! Gary Grayson" into a Google search box and select the Images option.

For more about philosophers' views on the purpose of art, see https://en.wikipedia.org/wiki/Art#Purpose

D: SCIENCE AND NATURE

Is scientific truth the only sort there is? How is science different from magic? Is nature our friend or our enemy? Can science foretell the future? Is genetic engineering wrong? These are the sorts of questions tackled by the philosophy of science.

Philosophers disagree about these and many other questions. For example:

- **Positivists** think that scientific truth is the only sort of truth, and everything else is mere opinion.

- **Realists** think that science investigates a world that really is there, just as we see it, whereas non-realists think we construct this world rather than just looking at it.

- Some think it is our vocation to **control** nature, whereas others think we should try to live in **harmony** with it.

We shall find examples of these types of philosopher in the pages that follow. Time to dive in and meet them!

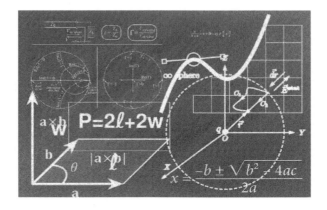

15. Will the sun rise tomorrow?

Phoebe, the more intellectual of the Terrible Twins, has been reading up on the 18th Century philosopher David Hume. It has made her very worried.

'What's the matter with you today?' asks Philip, her more down-to-earth sibling, with a notable lack of sympathy.

'I'm worried that the sun won't rise tomorrow morning and we'll all freeze to death,' wails Phoebe piteously, tears welling up in her eyes.

'Oh, for goodness sake!' snaps the ever-practical Philip. 'Listen! The sun has risen every day for thousands of years, so of course it will rise tomorrow. It's obvious. Stop worrying and pull yourself together!'

'But how do I know ... the future ... will be the same ... as the past?' stammers Phoebe between sobs. 'Perhaps it's just about to change and we'll all die. Waaaahhhh!'

Philip stares at her, scarcely able to believe his eyes. 'Sisters!' he grumbles. 'It's about time she stopped reading philosophy. It's obviously not good for her!'

*   *   *

Can you set Phoebe's mind at rest? Can you prove to her that the sun will rise tomorrow morning as usual? Or are we not sure that it will?

When you have thought about this problem carefully, turn to the next page.

The future and the past

The sun has always risen in the past, but does that mean it will rise tomorrow morning?

The book which Phoebe is reading is called *An Enquiry Concerning Human Understanding* by David Hume, an 18th Century Scottish philosopher. Hume was an **empiricist**. Empiricists believe that all real knowledge is based on the evidence of our senses.

Hume points out that we only have evidence from our senses about how the world works in the present and the past. Obviously, we have no evidence about the future because it hasn't happened yet. So, we cannot be sure what the future will bring. We cannot even be sure that the sun will rise tomorrow.

Most people get round this problem in the way that Philip suggests. For the last several thousand years the sun has always risen as usual, they say, so obviously it will do so tomorrow as well. But this is a circular argument. You must *believe* that the future will behave in the same way as the past to *prove* that it will. You assume what you are supposed to be proving.

What evidence is there for this belief about the world staying the same? There is a lot of evidence for it being true *in the past*. We know that nature behaved the same way in 2001 CE as it did in 2000 CE, for example, because we were there watching it. And the same is true for 2002 compared with 2001. So, *in the past*, the future has always turned out to be the same as the earlier past.

But will this continue? Can we be sure it will behave the same way in 2022 as it currently does in 2021? No, we cannot be *sure*, says Hume. We will just have to wait and see.

*　　*　　*

Once you have understood Hume's argument, there is extraordinarily little chance of proving it wrong. Phoebe has seen this, and that is why she is so worried. She is correct; it is impossible to *prove* that the sun will rise tomorrow morning.

But perhaps she is overreacting by being so worried. There are lots of other things that are more likely to give us trouble than the failure of the sun to rise (global warming, financial crises, pandemics, terrorism), so perhaps she is worrying about the wrong thing? And anyway, isn't it better to be excited about the future being different, rather than worried?

So, although Phoebe is philosophically more correct, Philip has a more sensible approach to life in an uncertain world. As Hume himself says, at the end of his book: there comes a point where you just have to give up such philosophical thoughts and simply get on with life.

Three extra questions for budding philosophers

Here are some related puzzles with which to test your friends, family, and teachers. There are some hints about them in the Commentary at the back of the book.

1. Science is based on experiments using sense experience. So, can science predict the future?

2. Why do scientific laws stay the same year after year? Why don't they change like everything else?

3. Which matters more: security or adventure?

Further research online

You can read the relevant section of Hume's book online for yourself by following this link and finding Section 4:
https://davidhume.org/texts/e/

16. Has science found the truth?

Philip was reading about the Ancient Greeks the other day and he was not impressed by their early attempts at chemistry.

'You won't believe this,' he chuckled to his twin sister Phoebe. 'They actually believed are only four elements: air, earth, fire and water. What a silly idea! Everyone knows those aren't elements at all.' He was feeling very smug and superior.

Phoebe was a bit more sympathetic to the ancients. 'Well, an "element" is a material you can't split up into anything simpler. And they couldn't split up air or water, so of course they thought they were elements. It's not silly at all, just wrong.'

'Well, we know now that air and water aren't elements,' retorted Philip. 'We know the truth about elements and stuff, not made-up stories like in the old days.'

'So how do you know that in 3020 people won't laugh at the silly things you believe today?' asked Phoebe. 'After all, if science got it wrong in the past, how do we know it's got it right this time?'

'Oh nonsense,' grumbled Philip, wandering off to play with his chemistry set.

*   *   *

Who is right, Philip or Phoebe?

How can we be sure science has finally discovered the truth about the world, despite its many mistakes in the past?

When you have thought about this problem carefully, turn to the next page.

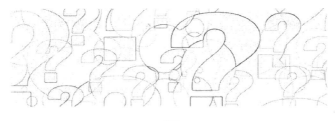

Scientific revolutions

Science got many things wrong in the past. So how do we know it is right today? Might it not change its mind again in the future?

In 1962, the philosopher **Thomas Kuhn** pointed out that science completely changes its mind now and then and starts again from scratch. He called these major events "scientific revolutions".

Astronomy gives a good example. Up to about 1500 CE, most scientists (including most Ancient Greeks) believed that the stars, planets and Sun revolve around the Earth. This is sensible: when you look up you see these bodies moving across the sky as if they are going around us.

However, in the 1540s the astronomer **Copernicus** suggested that the Earth and the other planets revolve around the Sun instead. And the stars only *seem* to move, he suggested, because the Earth spins on its axis beneath us. When Copernicus convinced other scientists he was right, the whole structure of astronomy collapsed and was rebuilt differently.

Now, said Kuhn, because this happens in science from time to time, we can never be sure another scientific revolution isn't just around the corner. So, everything that science currently believes *may* turn out to be false.

Other philosophers disagree with Kuhn. They think the job of science is not to *describe* the world but to *predict* how it *behaves*. When there is one of Kuhn's revolutions, although the description of the world changes completely, that doesn't matter too much. The old picture was quite good at predicting the behaviour of the world, so it was almost true. The new picture predicts it better, so it is more true. Science really does advance – really does get closer and closer to the truth – because it gets better and better at predicting how the world behaves. It doesn't really start again from scratch each time there is a scientific revolution.

So, maybe in the future chemistry will abandon the idea of elements completely. Who knows? But the current theory does a good job of predicting what will happen when you mix chemicals together. And that means it is at least partly – if not completely – true.

Three extra questions for budding philosophers

Here are some related puzzles with which to test your friends, family, and teachers. There are some hints about them in the Commentary at the back of the book.

1. The Ancient Greek philosopher Aristotle believed that objects fall down because they want to be nearer to the Earth. The later scientist Newton believed they fall because they are pulled by gravity. Which is the better theory, and why?

2. According to Newton (17th Century), light always travels in straight lines. According to Einstein (20th Century), very heavy objects bend space, so light curves around them. How could you find out whether Einstein is right?

3. On a dark night, you can see the Moon moving across the sky around you. It looks like it is moving, and it feels like the Earth is standing still. So, why believe otherwise?

Further research online

You can find out about Copernicus here:

https://en.wikipedia.org/wiki/Nicolaus_Copernicus

You can find some more examples of scientific revolutions here:

https://en.wikipedia.org/wiki/Paradigm_shift

Einstein

17. Is time travel possible?

Philip has been watching *Dr Who*, and he is excited about the possibility of time travel. 'The dinosaurs. Yes, I'd definitely like to see them. And the building of Stonehenge. Then maybe I'll go forwards to when I'm grown up and never come back. That'd be fun!'

Phoebe, his twin sister, sighs patiently. '*Dr Who* is only a story, Philip. You can't really travel backwards or forwards in time, you know. It's impossible.

'No, it isn't!' retorts her brother. 'Science says time is a fourth dimension, like length, breadth and height. So of course you can travel around in it. I'm going to make my own time machine, just like the Tardis!'

Phoebe sighs again. 'No, Philip. Time always goes forwards at the same speed, and we are stuck in it. You can't speed it up or slow it down, and you can't jump forwards or backwards. That's *proper* science, like we do at school.'

But Philip is not to have his dreams squashed so easily. He wanders off to sketch out a design for his time-travelling breakthrough. He'll show her!

*　　*　　*

Who is right? Will Philip really be able to build his own version of the Tardis? Or is that impossible, as Phoebe thinks? When you have thought about this problem carefully, turn to the next page.

Will Philip really be able to build his own version of the Tardis and travel in time? That depends on what "time" actually is and how it behaves – which is less clear than you might think.

Here are two surprising ideas about time that important thinkers have come up with.

Kant

The philosopher **Immanuel Kant** (1724 – 1804) believed that "time" (along with "space" and "cause") is something that our minds add to the world rather than it actually being there outside our heads. He argued that the raw data we receive through our eyes is simply a meaningless set of flashing lights, but that our minds organise it into an ordered world by fitting it into a time framework of our own making. If this is true (and it is hard to prove it is not) then time travel could only be something that happens in our heads, not out there in the real world. In other words, it could only be an illusion, like a dream or a fantasy.

Einstein

The physicist **Albert Einstein** (1879 – 1955) denied that time always goes at the same speed, or that events necessarily happen in the order they appear to.

Consider a boy and a girl on different planets who both drop a ball together. The girl drops her ball, but sees the boy drop his ball *some minutes later* when the light from that event reaches her. So, she believes she dropped her ball first. But the boy believes the opposite: he only sees the girl drop her ball when light reaches him from *her* planet. So which event happened first? Or did they happen at the same time? The answer depends on where you are standing, and there is no place to choose which gives you the "right" answer to that question. This is part of Einstein's famous theory of **relativity**.

Einstein's theory also predicts a strange thing that has been verified by experiment: that time goes faster or slower depending on how quickly you are moving. If I see a clock on a spaceship which is moving past me very fast, the clock seems to be running slower than my own clock. So, if Phoebe sends Philip off on an extremely fast journey to a distant star and back again, she will see his clock run slower throughout the journey. When he gets back, he will be several years younger than his twin sister! Philip and Phoebe will have moved through time at different speeds. And in that sense Philip will have achieved time travel.

But can Philip really make a Tardis and visit the dinosaurs in the past, or visit the distant future before it happens? Unfortunately not. Philip has been misled by talk of time as a "fourth dimension". You cannot travel around in it like you can travel around in space.

On the other hand, Phoebe is also wrong that time is a mysterious "something" that flows evenly onwards for everyone, everywhere, at the same speed. Whatever it is, it is more complicated than that.

Three extra questions for budding philosophers

Here are some related puzzles with which to test your friends, family, and teachers. There are some hints about them in the Commentary at the back of the book.

1. When you are bored, time seems to go more slowly. Does it really?

2. In the "dropping balls" case above, what does it mean to say that the two people dropped their balls "together"?

3. We measure time using a clock. But how do we know that our clock is running at a steady speed? We might say: by comparing it with other clocks. But how do we know *all* the clocks in the world are not speeding up or slowing down?

Further research online

You can read more about Einstein's theory of relativity here:

https://plus.maths.org/content/whats-so-special-about-special-relativity

18. Nature: guide or threat?

Phoebe is daydreaming about an earlier time, before the invention of cities, cars, and computers, when people lived in harmony with nature. Following the cycles of the sun, moon, and stars, immersed in the natural rhythms of the seasons, they must have been so happy, she thinks.

'Sentimental twaddle!' breaks in Philip, her ever-practical twin brother. 'Follow nature? Pah! All that gave people in the old days was disease, pain, and an early death. We don't need to *follow* nature; we need to keep it *under control*. Give nature half a chance and it'll destroy us: floods, storms, droughts, famines, volcanoes, plagues … Nature is our enemy; there's nothing good about it.'

Phoebe is not convinced. 'But we're part of nature ourselves, Philip, so how can it be our enemy? Surely nature's ways *must* best. Fighting nature would be fighting ourselves – how is that ever going to work?'

*　　*　　*

Who is right? Is nature our wise friend and guide, as Phoebe believes? Or is it a threatening enemy, as Philip thinks? Should we follow nature, or fight to control it?

When you have thought about this problem carefully, turn to the next page.

Is nature our wise friend and guide, or a threatening enemy? Should we follow nature, or fight to control it?

Different sorts of nature

If we decide to follow nature, we hit a snag. Which aspect of nature should be our guide? There are many different possibilities.

Human nature

First, there are own natural drives – our feelings and needs – which we call "human nature". It makes sense to satisfy these drives if we can, because denying them is likely to make us unhappy and less productive. For example, human beings are naturally competitive. So, it is probably better to harness this competitiveness to produce higher achievement at work and in sports, rather than try to get rid of it completely.

However, human nature also includes some very unpleasant things, such as selfishness, greed, and violence. We must control these, not give in to them. So following "human nature" completely could get us into serious trouble.

Natural selection

Second, life on our planet has been governed by "natural selection" since its origins millions of years ago. Natural selection means that only the strong survive long enough to reproduce, while the weak die young. This keeps species healthy and well-adapted to their environments, and it has driven evolution to produce more advanced species like our own. So perhaps we should follow this aspect of nature, celebrating the strong ones among us and letting the weak ones simply perish?

But this would mean shutting the National Health Service, leaving ill babies and old people to die, scrapping state benefits for those who fall on hard times, and abandoning many other humane aspects of our civilisation. Do we *really* want to live in a society like that, even if we are one of the strong ones?

Cycles and seasons

Third, nature, and our own bodies, have a range of natural cycles – such as the seasons and our "body clocks". We generally do better if we pay attention to these cycles rather than fighting against them. We cannot work efficiently for 24 hours at a stretch, for example, because our bodies have a natural need for periodic sleep. Nor is it sensible to ignore the seasons and try to play cricket outside in an English February.

However, sometimes we must ignore these natural cycles for the greater good. We need nurses and firefighters working at night, for example, when "naturally" they should be asleep. And we light our houses in the evenings during winter, when "naturally" we should be sitting in darkness.

Nature and civilisation

Civilisation has progressed by controlling nature rather than by following it. Here are three examples. All are important and all are "unnatural":

- Wearing clothes and heating houses. This keeps the temperature next to our skins comfortable all over the world at every time of year. Naturally, we could only survive in the tropics.

- Flood defences and drainage schemes. These make it possible to live and to grow crops in areas which would otherwise be under water, such as Holland and the Somerset Levels.

- Weeding fields, killing pests and refrigerating food. These make it possible to produce and keep enough food to feed us throughout the year.

However, it is generally more effective to work with nature where we can. For example:

- Using natural predators to control pests often works better than applying lots of insecticide.

73

- Building houses on high ground, rather than on flood plains, is wiser in the long run.

In fact, ignoring nature completely tends to backfire and hurt us eventually.

Both/and, not either/or

So, in the end, nature is neither *just* a wise guide nor *just* a threat, but a bit of both. We can neither simply beat it down, nor just follow it, if we want to thrive.

The wisest people and civilisations are the ones that go with nature when they can but overrule it when they must.

Phoebe and Philip are both right – partly.

Three extra questions for budding philosophers

Here are some related puzzles with which to test your friends, family, and teachers. There are some hints about them in the Commentary at the back of the book.

1. Is selfishness natural? Is it wrong?

2. Natural selection keeps a species healthy, but it is cruel. Which matters more, health or kindness?

3. If we are part of nature, how can anything we do or make be "unnatural"?

Further research online

To explore the different meanings of "nature", see:

https://en.wikipedia.org/wiki/Nature

For an unusual and interesting view of the Earth and its natural systems, see:

https://en.wikipedia.org/wiki/Gaia_hypothesis

19. Magic, science and technology

'Magic? Don't be silly! Everyone knows that science has disproved that sort of thing. Nobody believes in magic these days.' Philip is being at his most superior.

But Phoebe is reading about the ancient Egyptians, and she finds their belief in magic quite attractive. 'I don't know, Philip. Surely Science can't explain *everything*? And if magic never worked, why did people ever believe that it did?'

'Oh, that's just because science hadn't been invented yet,' her brother replies loftily. Now we can do actual *experiments* to find things out. And if you want something done you use technology, not *spells*. Anyway, you don't make someone by better by doing silly rituals. You give them proper medicines instead.'

Well, Phoebe certainly agrees that modern doctors are good at curing people, and that engineers are good at building bridges; but she is not willing to give up on magic entirely. How about the time she had made a wish after seeing a shooting star in the sky and it came true? Philip's view of the universe seems a bit – well – lacking in *magic* somehow.

'Oh, nonsense' snorts Philip, stomping off to play with his computer.

*   *   *

Who is right? Is Philip correct that magic is now completely out of date because science and technology have replaced it? Or is Phoebe right that this misses something important?

When you have thought about this problem carefully, turn to the next page.

Is Philip correct that science and technology have completely replaced magic? Or is Phoebe right that this view of the matter misses something important?

The standard answer

Philip is correct about one thing. In ancient times, human beings had not yet discovered how nature works, so could not predict or control its behaviour reliably. Modern science has now done just that.

We now know the rules which moving objects follow (physics), how and why different substances react together (chemistry) and why people die of diseases (biology). This knowledge helps us manipulate the world for our own benefit much more effectively than ancient humans could.

As a result, we no longer need to resort to spells or charms if people get ill or believe that rituals can make it rain.

But is that an end of the matter? Is magic now just simply out of date? Perhaps not, for three reasons.

Science and psychology

First, the world we live in and see is partly a creation of our own minds. Just think about how differently the world looks and feels when you are in a good or a bad mood, depressed or joyful. If your mind changes, so does the world you live in.

Now, magic may or may not change how atoms move about outside our heads, but it can certainly change how we think and feel. If we make a wish on a falling star (as Phoebe did) we become more hopeful and the world brightens up a little. And if we feel more hopeful, we are more likely to act in a positive way, changing the future for the better. So, in this sense, magic can "work".

Magic and the magical

Second, people sometimes describe special times and places as "magical", meaning they are different from the ordinary, run-of-the-mill world. Think about how you feel on Christmas Eve, for example, or when in a secret place in nature that is precious to you. On these occasions you seem to be in a different, enchanted universe.

This is something science finds extremely hard to cope with. For science, all times and all places are the same and behave in the same way. Science does not believe in "special" – and hence it does not believe in "magical" either.

But doesn't science miss something important because of this?

Spells and causes

Third, science insists that all events can be traced back to physical causes. But many events are far too complex for science to be able to show how this works. It deals happily with simple situations, like what will happen when one billiard ball hits another, or when two chemicals are mixed and heated. But what of, say, a driver who makes a wish (or casts a spell) to help them find a parking space in a busy street? Science believes this cannot work. But some people insist that it does.

This case is too complicated to analyse completely in terms of causes and their effects. Yes, making the wish may make the person more relaxed and hopeful, which might change how they behave and might increase their chance of success. It will also affect other people, who will react to our now-relaxed driver differently. But can we be sure exactly what is going on in this situation, or if, in fact, the chances of our driver getting parked are really increased?

It is impossible to carry out a scientific experiment to prove or disprove this spell's effectiveness – because the attitude of the spell-caster is different when being tested.

*   *   *

So, whether you believe that wishes and spells are effective is partly a matter of faith. You either believe they can work, or you do not.

Is magic out of date? Watch yourself carefully over the next few days to see if you *really* believe it is.

Three extra questions for budding philosophers

Here are some related puzzles with which to test your friends, family, and teachers. There are some hints about them in the Commentary at the back of the book.

1. What is the difference between "magic" as discussed above and "magical tricks" as performed by a stage magician?

2. What is the difference, if any, between a religious person praying and someone performing a magical spell?

3. Professional sportspeople often perform simple rituals, or wear certain things, to "bring them luck". Is this magic? Can it work?

Further research online

Find out about different theories of the relationship between science, magic, and religion here:

https://en.wikipedia.org/wiki/Magic_(supernatural)#Theories_on_t he_relationship_of_magic.2C_science.2C_art_and_religion

E: PEOPLE AND SOCIETY

Are real friends people who do what you want? How much should different jobs be paid? Can society be completely free and equal? Is happiness the only thing that matters? These are the sorts of questions tackled by social and political philosophy.

Philosophers disagree about these and many other questions. For example:

- Some **Socialists** think that everyone should be paid equally, while **classical liberals** think people should be rewarded according to their abilities and efforts.

- **Utilitarians** think the best thing to achieve is the greatest happiness for the greatest number of people, while **Kantians** think that doing your duty is more important.

- **Existentialists** believe that freedom is extremely important, while philosophers like **Hobbes** argue that law and order matters more.

We shall find examples of these types of philosopher in the pages that follow. Time to dive in and meet them!

20. The Mars colony

Philip and Phoebe, the terrible twins, rarely if ever agree. Yesterday they were discussing how much people should be paid for the jobs they do.

'I think everyone should be paid the same,' said Phoebe. 'Surely that's fair. Why should anyone be paid extra when we are all just people?'

'But some people might have to work harder than others,' replied Philip. 'Or they might have more unpleasant or dangerous jobs, or they might be cleverer and be able to do more important work.'

'I suppose so,' Phoebe conceded reluctantly. But if we *are* going to pay people differently, I think we should pay the carers extra – the nurses, teachers and so on. They do the most important jobs.'

'No, they don't,' Philip retorted. 'What about the people in charge, like the Prime Minister and the CEOs of big companies? They are far more important.'

'Hmm', said Phoebe. 'What if there was a brand new colony starting up on Mars. I wonder how they'd decide who gets paid what?'

'I'll tell you one thing,' said Philip. 'You'd never get them to agree. Everyone always thinks they deserve more than other people. It's human nature to think that way.'

*   *   *

Should everyone in The Mars Colony be paid the same? If not, who should be paid the most and why?

Is there any way we could get the colonists to agree about this?

When you have thought about these problems carefully, turn to the next page.

80

The veil of ignorance

Should everyone in The Mars Colony be paid the same? If not, who should be paid the most and why?

Is there any way we could get the colonists to agree about this?

An American philosopher called **John Rawls** suggests an answer to the last of these questions in a book called *A Theory of Justice* (1971).

Philip is correct, of course, that we all see our own needs much more clearly than we see the needs of anyone else. So, left to our own devices, our natural selfishness means we will vote ourselves the most money in The Mars Colony.

To avoid this, Rawls suggests the colonists should hold a meeting before leaving Earth. They should be given a list of jobs in the Colony and be asked to decide what each job should be paid, but with one crucial condition: **none of them would yet know which job they were going to get**. This would neutralise their natural selfishness and make them decide fairly what each job is worth. Maybe they would even play safe by awarding everyone the same pay.

Rawls calls this operating "behind a **veil of ignorance**", and he thinks that it would produce a more just (fair) society if used widely.

You could try out Rawls' idea next time you have to divide up some jobs that no one really wants to do. Get everyone to agree on equal packages of jobs, and *then* draw lots to decide who gets which package. This will stop anyone selfishly giving themselves an easy time.

Rawls believes, like Phoebe, that everyone in society should be treated equally. But he thinks we should pay some people more than others in one circumstance: if it will help the whole of society, especially its most disadvantaged members.

For example, we should pay doctors more than road sweepers, because otherwise no one will go through the long training to

81

become a doctor, and there will be no medical care. The doctors' greater income benefits, not only themselves, but all of society. Including the road sweepers, since it permits them to get medical care.

Three extra tricky questions for budding philosophers:

1. Karl Marx suggested the principle: 'From each according to his ability; to each according to his needs.' Is this fair?
2. Who deserves the most pay and why: a doctor, a footballer, a factory-owner or a soldier?
3. How *is* it decided who gets what in the UK, and does this produce a fair result?

Further research

You can find out more about John Rawls and his ideas on this internet page:

https://en.wikipedia.org/wiki/A_Theory_of_Justice

21. Philip's Fantastic Friends

Philip has come up with a brilliant idea for making lots of money. He is going to design, patent and sell machines called "Philip's Fantastic Friends".

The Fantastic Friend will be an improvement on normal, human friends in various important ways. It will be a better listener, for a start, giving you its full interest and attention for hours at a time if necessary. It will always laugh at your jokes, and it will never get grumpy, bored, or tired.

The Friend will be programmed always to agree with you – unless you don't want it to, of course, in which case it will argue against you resourcefully before finally admitting that were right all along. It will be full of bright ideas for what to do but will always fall happily in line with what you choose.

Most importantly of all, the Friend will always like you, and will never fall out with you.

Philip thinks his idea is a winner, but he is meeting a bit of consumer resistance from his twin sister.

'What a *stupid* idea!' complains Phoebe. 'Only a *boy* could think that would be a *real* friend! I want a proper person as my friend, not some machine that has been programmed to like me!'

*   *   *

Would the Fantastic Friend be an improvement on human friends, as Philip thinks, or not a real friend at all? When you have thought about this problem carefully, turn to the next page.

Would Philip's Fantastic Friends be an improvement?

What is a genuine friend? Is it someone who always does what you want and thinks you are wonderful? Or is it more complicated than that?

You might think that Philip is right. After all, a faithful dog is rather like one of the Fantastic Friends, and aren't dogs said to be "man's best friend?" Dogs are loyal, adoring, always pleased to see you, and always willing to fall in with your plans. They do not go off you, as normal friends sometimes do, and they still love you even if you find it difficult to make human friends. But yet …

In 1807, the German philosopher **Hegel** published an important book translated into English as *Phenomenology of Spirit*. The book is extremely difficult to understand, even for professional philosophers, but one small section has caught people's imaginations ever since. It is known as **the Master-Slave dialectic**.

Hegel said we are only fulfilled when we are "recognized" – valued and appreciated – by someone else. This is one reason why solitary confinement is such a terrible punishment for human beings. But who does this "someone else" need to be?

You might think that, if a master has a slave, the master will get that recognition from his slave. After all, the slave always does what the master wants and must be pleasant to him. But there is a problem. Because the slave is not the master's equal, he is not, from the master's perspective, a proper person at all. So, although the slave recognizes him, the master is not being recognized by a proper "someone else" and he is not fulfilled by the relationship.

On the other hand, the slave certainly experiences the master as a proper person. The master seems equal to – in fact greater than – himself. So, if the slave earns his master's approval, he will feel fulfilled by the relationship.

This is a **paradox** – a seemingly absurd idea which turns out to be true. The slave, despite not being in control, gets more genuine satisfaction out of the relationship than the master. Just as a faithful dog is fulfilled by being devoted to its loving master, while its master needs a relationship with a human equal as well.

So, sorry Philip. The Fantastic Friends may catch on as a replacement for dogs, but not as replacements for genuine human friends – exactly because they always do what we want. Phoebe is right: human friends may be difficult, but we need them. Without them we get lonely.

Three extra questions for budding philosophers

Here are some related puzzles with which to test your friends, family, and teachers. There are some hints about them in the Commentary at the back of the book.

1. What matters more in sport, and why: winning, or having a good battle with an equal?

2. Why are pop idols, with millions of adoring fans, so often unhappy?

3. Theologians sometimes suggest that God made people because he was lonely. Is this a sensible suggestion?

Further research online

You can find out more about Hegel and his theories starting here:

https://en.wikipedia.org/wiki/Master%E2%80%93slave_dialectic

22. The Happiness Machine

Philip sat in front of The Happiness Machine and wondered what to do.

If he pushed the button, he would be taken permanently to a virtual reality world in which he would be completely happy. Once inside, he would have no idea he was only in a virtual world and that the events happening to him were unreal. It would seem just as if he were living an ordinary life, but as one of the "winners" for which everything goes right.

It was an extremely attractive idea. Paradise awaited.

'No, Philip. No!' protested Phoebe. 'It'll just be a phoney world, a bogus paradise. Nothing that you do in there will be real at all. You'll be wasting your life!'

True. But did that matter? Philip was not sure. And he had to make up his mind, or his chance would be lost forever …

*   *   *

Should Philip push the button and enter the phoney world of The Happiness Machine? Or should he stay outside in the real world, with all its disappointments and suffering?

When you have thought about this problem carefully, turn to the next page.

Should Philip push the button and enter the phoney world of The Happiness Machine? Before advising him, we need to consider three things.

How important is happiness?

Is happiness the only thing that matters? Parents often say they do not mind what their children do provided they are happy, but is this right?

Utilitarian philosophers think that only happiness matters. According to them, the right thing to do is whatever leads to the greatest happiness. So, provided everyone could have their own Happiness Machine, they might advise everyone to push the button.

But other philosophers reject this. Better to do the honourable, courageous, caring, or dutiful thing and be miserable, they say, than to be happy after doing something wrong. And entering a phoney world would be wrong – it would be giving up on our real, human life.

What does happiness mean?

The original Utilitarians thought of happiness as the presence of pleasure and the absence of pain. But we all know that we need more than pleasure to satisfy us.

We also need challenges to overcome, a sense of life's meaning, goals to aim for, and people to love. Which is why people do painful things like climb mountains, train as athletes, or sacrifice themselves for their children. These people trade in short-term pain for long-term satisfaction.

Could The Happiness Machine deliver these things as well? Perhaps so, but its programme would need to be extraordinarily complex.

Can we be truly happy without times of unhappiness?

Wouldn't being happy all the time end up being rather boring?

Don't the best feelings often come immediately after an escape from painful times – the relief that you feel when toothache wears off, or the pleasure of eating after you have spent a long time hungry?

Would such painful times need to built into the Machine's programme as well? In which case, the virtual world is beginning to sound an awful lot like normal life!

*   *   *

So, should Philip press the button?

Perhaps not – at least not without doing some more research. He should think carefully about the type of happiness that the Machine offers, and he should consider the other things in life that matter as well.

The Happiness Machine is certainly attractive. But it is unlikely to give him the paradise that it claims on the box.

Three extra questions for budding philosophers

Here are some related puzzles with which to test your friends, family, and teachers. There are some hints about them in the Commentary at the back of the book.

1. Which matters more – developing your character, or having a good time?

2. Can you be sure you are not living inside a virtual reality world right now?

3. Which is better – a happy pig or an unhappy philosopher?

Further research online

For more about the meaning of happiness, see https://en.wikipedia.org/wiki/Happiness

23. Can society be free and equal?

'*Liberté, égalité, fraternité* (freedom, equality, brotherhood) – aren't those a wonderful set of ideals, Philip?' Phoebe's eyes are shining as she tries to enthuse her twin brother with principles of the French Revolution of 1789.

'Hmph! There wasn't much freedom for the people who disagreed with the revolutionaries, was there?' asks a sceptical Philip. 'More than 41,000 people executed by guillotine during The Reign of Terror in 1793 – 1794; including a set of nuns simply for refusing to give up their vows. Not the sort of society I'd want to live in.'

'Yes, but that was after the revolution went wrong,' persists Phoebe. 'You surely can't argue with any of those three principles, can you? Everyone wants to be free; and surely everyone ought to be treated equally. It's so obvious!'

'Maybe so, but *I* don't think you can have all three at the same time. Give people freedom, and equality disappears. You can only *force* people to be equal, and that's not very brotherly.'

'Oh Philip!' sighs Phoebe impatiently. 'Why can't you use your imagination? Just because it has never happened in the past, it doesn't mean it's impossible in the future.'

*   *   *

Who is right? Is Phoebe correct that a free and equal society is within our grasp? Or is Philip right that both at the same time is simply impossible? When you have thought about this problem carefully, turn to the next page.

Is Phoebe correct that a free and equal society is achievable? Or is Philip right that getting both at the same time is impossible?

A lot depends upon what we mean by "equality" and by "freedom".

Equality

To say we want people to be "equal" can mean at least four different things. From the least achievable to the most achievable, these are:

Equality of ability. This is unachievable. Some people are just more talented than others. No amount of training or education can eliminate this completely, although it can make the differences less severe.

Equality of outcomes. This is the idea that everyone in society should have the same amount of money, or the same amount of success. It can almost be achieved, but only by holding back the most talented and spending a huge amount of money helping the least talented. Our tax and benefits system goes some way to reducing the differences in peoples' wealth.

Equality of opportunity. This is the idea that everyone should have the same chance in life, and that what you make of this should be down to your own efforts and abilities. Again, the disadvantaged need a lot of money and help from the state to bring this about.

Equality under the law. This is the idea that everyone – rich or poor, black or white, male or female – should have the law applied to them in the same way. This is possible, given continued effort to root out corruption and discrimination.

In the UK, the fourth version of equality is something which everyone accepts, while the third is something we struggle to achieve as far as it is possible.

Freedom

To say we want people to be "free" can also mean several different things. Two possible meanings of freedom are:

90

Freedom to do whatever I want. This is unattainable. I may want to run a mile in 3 minutes, or to visit planets around other stars, but these are impossible goals given that I am a human being living in the early 21st Century.

Freedom under the law. This is the ability to do whatever I can, provided I have enough money and it does not harm anyone else.

In the UK, the second is a form of freedom we believe everyone should have.

The French Revolution

The French Revolution of 1789 started off with high ideals, as Phoebe has discovered. These were stated in a document called *The Declaration of the Rights of Man and of the Citizen*. This opened with the phrase 'Men are born free and equal in rights,' and included this key section:

> Liberty consists in the freedom to do everything which injures no one else; hence the exercise of the natural rights of each man has no limits except those which assure to the other members of the society the enjoyment of the same rights.

As you can see, this includes the ideals of *freedom under the law* and *equality under the law.*

The problem came when the revolutionaries attempted to impose *equality of outcomes* by force. The original form of the slogan which has impressed Phoebe was '*Liberté, Égalité, Fraternité ou la Mort'* (Freedom, Equality, Brotherhood – or Death) and the last of these was often the price for trying to bring about the second.

Other idealistic societies – like the Communist societies of the 20th Century – run up against the same problem: you can only impose equality of outcomes by force, and this means a loss of freedom for many of the population.

So, Phoebe is right: freedom, equality and brotherhood are all wonderful things.

But Philip is also correct: some forms of equality can only be gained by a loss of freedom. At least, that seems to be the lesson of history.

Three extra questions for budding philosophers

Here are three related puzzles with which to test your friends, family, and teachers. There are some hints about them in the Commentary at the back of the book.

1. Which matters more: the freedom of individual people, or the good of society as a whole?

2. Should people be taxed equally, have equal amounts of money after taxation, or be free to decide how much tax they pay?

3. Should people be allowed to spend their money on private education or private healthcare if they want to?

Further research online

You can find the 1789 *Declaration of the Rights of Man and of the Citizen* here:

https://en.wikipedia.org/wiki/Declaration_of_the_Rights_of_Man_and_of_the_Citizen

http://upload.wikimedia.org/wikipedia/commons/b/b6/LibertyEqualityorDeath.jpg

24. Beam me up, Scotty!

You may have seen it on TV. Captain Kirk steps into the transporter room in the Starship Enterprise, the beam is energised, and seconds later he rematerialises down on the planet's surface. It would certainly beat the bus as a way of getting to school!

But hold on a minute. *What* is now down on the surface? Is it really Captain Kirk, or is it just a copy of him? Does the real Captain Kirk still exist?

As Philip and Phoebe, the terrible twins, rarely agree about anything, it is no surprise that they are at loggerheads about this as well.

'Of course it's Captain Kirk, silly!' says Philip. 'He looks exactly the same – he's even wearing the same clothes. *And* he behaves just like Captain Kirk. He even remembers being in charge up on the Enterprise. Anyway, if he isn't, where has the real Captain Kirk gone? There's no dead body anywhere.'

'Sorry, Philip,' reposts Phoebe, 'that's just not good enough. We could make an exact copy of Captain Kirk that looks and behaves just like the real thing. And if you got the copy's brain structure right, it would even "remember" being Captain Kirk earlier.'

'Humph,' says Philip. 'In that case, how do I know you're not just an imitation Phoebe?' And he stomps off to play with his computer.

*   *   *

Who is right? Is transporting in this way possible? And, if so, does the same person come out at the end? When you have thought about this problem carefully, turn to the next page.

Philip and Phoebe both want to know what makes a "transported" Captain Kirk the same man as the man who was previously on the Enterprise.

Here are two answers that do not work:

Two wrong answers

1. The man on the planet's surface looks, thinks, and behaves just like Captain Kirk. True. But someone who has a brain tumour may develop a different personality; and someone who is badly burned may look different, while still being the same person. So, something else which must be the same if the man on the planet is really Captain Kirk.

2. The man on the planet's surface remembers being Captain Kirk on the Enterprise. True. But it is possible to have "false memories" of events which did not happen. Phoebe is correct: memory is based on electrical charges and the structures and patterns of molecules in the brain. So, if a model was made with the correct charges and molecular structure it would *falsely* remember being Captain Kirk.

The identity problem

As Philip has spotted, the transporter problem should make him doubt whether the Phoebe he sees today is the same as the Phoebe he knew yesterday. Even more puzzling: why should he believe that *he* – Philip – is the same person that he remembers being yesterday?

Once again, there are two answers that don't work:

3. Unlike in the transporter case, Phoebe's body has been visible all the time. Philip could have watched it continuously to make sure it was not replaced by another one.

True. But the body does not contain exactly the same atoms that it did before, and over the course of several years remarkably few of these remain the same. So, is it the same body throughout? No. It is rather like the "genuine Saxon axe" which has had three new heads and four new handles.

4. Philip has been conscious since getting up this morning, so he is sure he is still the same person. True. But this does not apply when we go to sleep. So, why should he believe he is the same person that went to bed last night? Because he remembers yesterday? See 2 above. Because he looks and feels the same, and other people recognize him? See 1 above. Oh dear! Perhaps he *isn't* the same person after all!

Faced with this problem, philosophers have reacted in different ways. Descartes (see Puzzle 1) believed in a "soul" inside each of us, different from our bodies and our minds, that stays the same while everything else changes. So, if Captain Kirk's soul is present on the planet surface then the transporter has worked.

However, this soul is notoriously difficult to detect. Is there any such thing? Wittgenstein (see Puzzle 5) did not think so. He denied there is *anything* which stays the same throughout life, making us who we are.

But who, if either, is correct?

Three extra questions for budding philosophers

Here are three related puzzles with which to test your friends, family, and teachers. There are some hints about them in the Commentary at the back of the book.

1. Some people claim to remember events from "former lives". How could you test whether these claims are true?

2. If someone permanently loses consciousness, are they still a "person"? Would it be OK to let them die?

3. Some religions teach that, after death, we go to live in heaven. Why does the "transporter" problem make this difficult to believe?

Further research online

To investigate these problems further, go to:

https://en.wikipedia.org/wiki/Personal_identity

25. Does democracy matter?

In Britain, all adults can **vote** in **elections** to choose the government, a system called **democracy**. But is this the best way to decide who rules us? As Philip and Phoebe rarely agree about anything, it is no surprise they do not agree about this either.

'Of course democracy is best, silly!' says Philip. 'Look at all the countries in the world where people don't get the vote and they have a terrible time. You must be able to choose your own government, otherwise you end up with terrible tyranny. It's obvious.'

But Phoebe is not convinced. 'There are some pretty terrible democratic countries as well, you know. Having the vote doesn't do those places much good, does it? And there are plenty of good countries which are not democracies but are doing very well indeed, like China and Saudi Arabia. Personally, I can't see the point of having a vote at all.'

* * *

Who is right? Is it really better if people get to choose their own government in elections? Does democracy actually matter?

When you have thought about this problem carefully, turn to the next page.

Does it matter whether we have the vote and choose our own government? Philip thinks it does, but Phoebe disagrees.

Monarchy

Plato and **Hobbes** were two philosophers who disapproved of democracy. Both thought that **monarchy** – rule by a king or queen – was more effective. And both thought that *effective* government was more important than *choice*.

Plato, an Ancient Greek, thought that *good* government is what really matters. If you give people the vote, most of whom are selfish, short-sighted, and ignorant, you will not get a government that acts wisely, fairly, or in the long-term interests of all.

Better to appoint philosophers as unelected kings, thought Plato. As philosophers, they will be wise and long-sighted. If without close family or property, they will not act selfishly. The result will be wise government in the true interests of all the people.

Hobbes, a 17th C English philosopher, thought that *good* government is less important than *strong* government. What we need most, he said, is an effective ruler to keep law and order and fight off foreign invasion, so we can all get on with our lives. Our true concerns are earning a living and looking after our families. For this we need peace and security, not the ability to choose our rulers.

Democracy produces weak governments, Hobbes reasoned. Always looking forward nervously to the next election, a democratic government is too scared to do the tough and unpopular things necessary for our long-term good. But a strong monarch, unworried about being voted out of office, can do what he knows is right.

Of course, such monarchs may take a lot of wealth for themselves. But this is less undesirable than the breakdown of law and order that goes with weak government.

Democracy

Other philosophers have supported democracy, for two very different reasons.

Existentialists regard *choice* as the most important thing in life. It is even more important that I make my own choices, they say, than that I choose wisely. So, it is more important that I get to choose my own rulers than that I have ones which do the best job.

Others have pointed to a serious problem with unelected monarchs – you cannot get rid of bad ones. This, they say, outweighs the disadvantages suffered by democracy. As **Churchill**, Britain's great wartime leader, once wittily put it:

> Many forms of government have been tried … in this world of sin and woe …. Democracy is the worst form of government – except for all those other forms that have been tried from time to time.

Three extra questions for budding philosophers

Here are three related puzzles with which to test your friends, family, and teachers. There are some hints about them in the Commentary at the back of the book.

1. Which matters most: being rich, being free, or doing the right thing?

2. Should the vote be denied to people who are too young, too bad, or too unintelligent?

3. Is Democracy just a western way of looking at things, or is it important for all human beings?

Further research online

You can find out about Hobbes here:

https://en.wikipedia.org/wiki/Thomas_Hobbes

and about Plato here:

https://en.wikipedia.org/wiki/Plato#The_State

F: GOD AND RELIGION

Are miracles possible? Why is there suffering in the world? Has God got anything to do with what is right and wrong? Are some myths true? Can we prove that God exists? These are the sorts of questions tackled by the **philosophy of religion**.

Philosophers disagree about all these questions. For example:

- **Theists** believe that God exists, **atheists** believe that God does not exist, while **agnostics** believe it is impossible to prove this one way or the other.

- Some believe that right and wrong are decided by what God thinks, while others believe we can work right and wrong out without referring to God at all.

This is a very tricky branch of philosophy, which is why we have left it until last. Hopefully, by now you realise how difficult it is to be sure that you are right. People being sure they are right about religion has caused a lot of suffering in the past.

Please note: in this section, God is sometimes referred to as "he" for simplicity, as the western religions have traditionally thought of their God as male. But the divine, if it exists, must transcend gender.

26. The Euthyphro dilemma

Philip and Phoebe, the terrible twins, are disagreeing about where right and wrong come from. Phoebe believes in God and is sure that this gives the answer, but Philip is unconvinced.

'It's obvious,' says Phoebe. 'If God says something is right, then it just *is* right, and that's an end of the matter. God decides what is right and wrong, we don't.'

'So, what if God changes his mind?' counters Philip. 'Does right and wrong change? Anyway, how do we know the universe is ruled by a *good* God? Maybe God is bad, and it's our duty to stand up to him and tell him he's wrong sometimes.'

Phoebe counterattacks. 'So, are you saying that right and wrong are just there, and that God, like everyone else, has to toe the line? That's silly! How can right and wrong be *just there*? Where do they come from if God didn't make them?'

'Hummmph', replies Philip grumpily. 'I don't know, but I know *you're* wrong – that's all!'

*   *   *

Who is right, Philip or Phoebe?

Where do right and wrong come from? And what, if anything, has God got to do with it?

When you have thought about this problem carefully, turn to the next page.

Where do right and wrong come from?

Is something wrong because God says so, or does God say so because it *is* wrong? Philip and Phoebe are right to be puzzled about this problem because it has plagued philosophers ever since the time of the Ancient Greeks. Plato explored the problem in a work called *Euthyphro*, so it is sometimes called **The Euthyphro Dilemma**.

Socrates, Plato's hero, is talking to a man called Euthyphro who is on the way to court to prosecute his own father for murder. When questioned, Euthyphro claims it is right to do this because it is pleasing to the gods. Socrates responds:

> Is what is right, right because the gods approve of it? Or do the gods approve of it because it is right?

Which is precisely the issue Philip and Phoebe are arguing about.

Now, the Ancient Greeks believed in many gods. But the question is still just as tricky if you believe in a single God. Because if something is only right because God says so – if God decides right and wrong – then it seems to be arbitrary. In other words, it could be different, and it might change (Philip's case). On the other hand, if God does not decide it, where does it come from? How can something as important as right and wrong just "be there" (Phoebe's case)?

Many modern philosophers side with Philip. They drop the idea of God completely and, along with God, give up the idea of an eternal, fixed right and wrong that we must always obey. They believe we make up our own right and wrong as we go along, either as individuals or as societies, and that it changes over time. So, for example, in the ancient world both slavery and the lordship of men over women were accepted as normal. They were not "wrong" in the ancient world. But they are both wrong now because our opinions have changed.

This position is called **relativism**. The problem is: we lose the ability to criticise other people and societies. We may think that slavery and the oppression of women are wrong, for example, but relativists say they are only "wrong for us", not wrong for everyone. Are we willing to accept this?

Other philosophers side with Phoebe. They point out that the ancient Greek gods were quite human-like. They fell out and fought with each other and were often, like people, unpleasant characters. The idea that right and wrong are decided by this unsavoury crew is not appealing.

But modern western religions believe in a very different God who is wise, good, loving, unchanging and the creator of the universe. Having made human beings, this God knows and wants what is best for them. It is reasonable to believe that right and wrong are defined by what such a God thinks, and that they are unchanging.

A position like this is called **non-relativism**. The problem is: does such a God really exist? And if so, how do we find out what he, she or it thinks? For example, Islamist terrorists believe in a God and are sure they know what he wants – the death of all those who do not believe in him. Do we agree with them?

So, on this occasion, Philip and Phoebe will need to keep arguing. They are both correct about the weakness of the other's position, but neither has a secure position of their own.

Three extra questions for budding philosophers

Here are some related puzzles with which to test your friends, family, and teachers. There are some hints about them in the Commentary at the back of the book.

1. Is it possible to imagine a universe created and ruled by an all-powerful but evil God? How can we be sure that we do not live in such a universe?

2. Who should have the final say about right and wrong in society: individuals or the state?

3. Is slavery wrong? If so, why?

Further research online

You can read Plato's work *Euthyphro* for yourself here:

http://classics.mit.edu/Plato/euthyfro.1b.txt

Plato

27. Why do natural disasters happen?

Phoebe has been watching some scenes of a natural disaster on TV, and it has left her feeling both upset and puzzled. 'But why, Philip?' she asks her twin. 'Why do awful things like this happen? It seems so pointless and unfair. Those poor people.'

Philip is also upset by the scenes, but he isn't puzzled like Phoebe. 'There's no reason for it,' he says philosophically. 'Bad things just happen, that's all. We just need to be grateful it isn't us, and help out if we can. There's no point asking why.'

But Phoebe is not convinced. 'There must be a reason that things like this happen, Philip, even if we can't see what it is. Otherwise the world is just meaningless.'

'I know we'd *like* there to be a reason,' responds Philip. 'But that doesn't mean there *is*. All we can do is make the best of it and try to make life better for the people we care about.'

*   *   *

Who is right? Are there reasons terrible natural disasters happen, as Phoebe thinks? Or are they just a matter of meaningless chance, as her brother believes?

When you have thought about this problem carefully, turn to the next page.

Is there a reason why natural disasters happen? Or are events like this just a matter of chance?

We rarely do much soul-searching when *good* things happen. It is the *bad* things we want explained. But Phoebe's problem is really part of a bigger question: is there a reason *anything* happens, good or bad? Is there an overall plan to the universe and to our lives, or is there not?

Some philosophers answer "yes" to this question, while others answer "no".

The problem of evil

Some philosophers are also religious. Many religious people believe in a God who gives meaning and purpose to the universe and to our lives, and they see natural disasters as part of **the problem of evil**.

Christianity, for example, believes in an all-loving and all-powerful God who has our best interests at heart. So, it is very puzzled when disasters happen. Christianity has tried the following solutions to the problem of evil, but has not found any of them completely convincing:

- *All natural disasters are divine punishment for human wrongdoing.* But in that case, why do good people often suffer more than bad ones?

- *Natural disasters are the work of the devil.* But surely an all-powerful God should be able to thwart the designs such a being?

- *The hidden good which comes out of natural disasters outweighs their obvious evil.* But surely disasters are often simply destructive, especially for the people who die?

Blind chance

Other philosophers deny there is any overall plan to the world, or any divine intelligence behind it. They believe everything happens purely by chance, so it does not make sense to ask "Why?"

These philosophers believe we must create our own meaning – we we cannot find it there already. For example, they would say, by caring about other people we *make* them important – they have no "real" importance of their own.

Most people, like Phoebe, instinctively feel otherwise. But these philosophers believe most people are simply wrong.

Action and understanding

It is easy to get depressed when faced with natural disasters, but that does not help anyone, least of all the victims. What they really need is *action* – and most people feel better when they are doing something to help.

On the gravestone of the philosopher Karl Marx is written:

> The philosophers have only interpreted the world in various ways. *The point is to change it.*

The wisest people, religious and non-religious, prove the truth of that saying by helping when disaster strikes.

Three extra questions for budding philosophers

Here are some related puzzles with which to test your friends, family, and teachers. There are some hints about them in the Commentary at the back of the book.

1. What sort of good can come out of natural disasters? Does this good make the disasters worthwhile?

2. Can we *make* our own meaning and purpose for life, or do we need to *find* it outside ourselves?

3. Is it possible to believe in a powerful and loving God, given what the world is like?

Further research online

You can read more about the problem of evil in religion and philosophy here: https://en.wikipedia.org/wiki/Problem_of_evil

28. Has science disproved religion?

'Religion? Don't be silly! Science has disproved all that superstitious nonsense. Religion is all just fairy tales. Science gives us the *real* facts about the universe!'

Philip is being at his most superior, but his sister Phoebe is not completely convinced. After all, he has been certain like this in the past but also wrong.

'But look, Philip, well over half the people in the world still follow one of the main religions, and lots of them have science degrees. Even Einstein was a religious man – was he just being silly? Surely it's more complicated than that.'

'Oh, come *on!*' retorted Philip. 'How can you possibly believe that God made the world in six days now we've found out about the Big Bang and fossil dinosaurs? It's … it's just ridiculous!'

Philip is really warming to his theme now. 'And now that science has discovered the laws of nature, we don't need God to explain why things happen. Religion is just out of date. Science has disproved it.'

*   *   *

Is Philip correct that science has disproved religion, and that religion is now out of date? Or is Phoebe right to think this is too simple?

When you have thought about this problem carefully, turn to the next page.

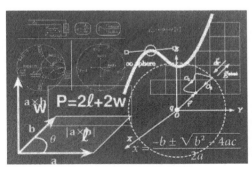

Is Philip correct that science has disproved religion, and that religion is simply out of date?

Although many people these days agree with him, Philip has made three major mistakes in what he says.

Buddhism

First, he assumes that "religion" is the same as Christianity and Judaism, which share a creation story in which God makes the world in six days. But there are several other major religions which believe no such thing.

Buddhism, for example, does not have a creator God at all, let alone one who takes only six days to do his work. So, showing that a god did not create the universe does not disprove religion as such.

History and myth

Second, many modern Christians and Jews do not take their Bible literally in the way that Philip implies. They understand that the Bible contains many **myths** – of which the creation story is one – which do not teach historical facts about the world in the way that geology does.

So, such people are quite happy to accept the Big Bang and the fossil dinosaurs – and indeed anything else which science discovers – but they still believe in God.

The meaning of life

Third, science and religion do not relate to each other in the way that Philip thinks. He sees religion as an old-fashioned version of science which has now been replaced by the real thing. But, in fact, science and religion talk about different things.

Science aims to find out *how* the world works. Its experiments discover how matter and energy behave so we can predict what will happen in the future and control the world better. It can tell us, for example, at what angle to fire a shell if we want to hit that target in the distance. Or how much hotter the world will get if we release a million extra tons of carbon dioxide into the air. Religion tells us nothing at all about this sort of thing.

Religion is about something quite different. It is about *why* the world is here at all, the real meaning of life, about how we should behave while we are alive, and how we can become happy. It tells us, for example, that caring for others is better than hating them, and that we really matter in the grand scheme of things. Science tells us nothing at all about this. It cannot tell us how to behave or why we are here – that is not its job.

Now, it may be that Philip is correct and that religion *is* out of date. But, if that is so, it is not because science has disproved it. Religion and science do not talk about the same things, so neither can prove the other false.

Phoebe is right – it is more complicated than Philip thinks.

Three extra questions for budding philosophers

Here are some related puzzles with which to test your friends, family, and teachers. There are some hints about them in the Commentary at the back of the book.

1. Science can tell you at what angle to fire a shell from a gun if you want to hit a target. Can it tell you whether it is right to fire the gun?

2. What scientific experiment, if any, could find out whether God exists?

3. Should religion be allowed to stop scientists carrying out certain experiments?

Further research online

You can discover more about the relationship between science and religion here:

https://en.wikipedia.org/wiki/Relationship_between_religion_and_science

109

29. Are miracles possible?

'It's a miracle!' Phoebe stares at her maths exam result in disbelief. 93% seems impossibly good.

'Don't be silly,' scoffs Philip. 'Miracles don't happen. They're against the laws of nature. You were just lucky, that's all.'

But Phoebe is not convinced. It feels too much like God stepping in to help her out for that. 'But I didn't even understand the questions. *And* I was ill the night before, so I couldn't revise properly. Someone must have been looking after me, I'm sure of it.'

'Look, there will be a simple explanation if you think carefully enough,' replies her sceptical brother. There's no need to bring God into it just because something unexpected and good has happened. Nice things are bound to happen to people sometimes – it doesn't mean that God has intervened when they do.'

*   *   *

Who is right? Should Phoebe feel grateful to God, or the Universe, for giving her an unexpected gift? Or should she agree with Philip that it is just a matter of chance?

When you have thought about this problem carefully, turn to the next page.

Do miracles ever happen? Or can unexpectedly good events always be explained in some other way?

Hume on miracles

The philosopher David Hume argued against believing in miracles in *An Enquiry Concerning Human Understanding* published in 1748.

A miracle involves breaking the laws of nature, he wrote. And, as these laws have been firmly established by experience, it is always more likely that an alleged miracle has occurred in some other way.

Imagine that someone tells you she saw a dead man raised back to life. It is much more likely that she is mistaken, or is deliberately lying to you, than that the event actually occurred.

Philip is siding with Hume in his argument with Phoebe.

Counter arguments

But there are two problems with Hume's position.

First, we are not sure what "the laws of nature" actually are. Scientists change their minds about them over the years, which makes Hume sound much too confident about our knowledge of them.

Second, when people use the word "miracle" they are not interested in whether the laws of nature have been broken at all.

For example, imagine a couple whose daughter is dying of leukaemia (a fatal blood disease). They pray that she will be cured and, after a lengthy course of treatment in hospital, she is.

This couple experience their daughter's healing as an answer to their prayers, and therefore as a miracle. They are not concerned about whether any laws of nature have been broken in making her better. They are just grateful that she is better, and experience that as a gift, not as a matter of chance.

111

This is what Phoebe meant by the result of her maths exam being a miracle. She feels grateful, whatever the reason for it.

*   *   *

So – do miracles ever happen?

In Phoebe's sense, all the time. In Philip's sense, who knows? Whenever you hear the word "miracle", always ask yourself what the speaker means by it.

Three extra questions for budding philosophers

Here are some related puzzles with which to test your friends, family, and teachers. There are some hints about them in the Commentary at the back of the book.

1. How can we be sure that today's "laws of nature" will not be disproved by science tomorrow?

2. 'Miracle goal saves Man. U.' What does the word "miracle" mean here?

3. 'There is no testimony that is sufficient to establish a miracle.' (David Hume) Is Hume right?

Further research online

You can read more about David Hume and miracles here:

https://en.wikipedia.org/wiki/David_Hume#Problem_of_miracles

30. Can we prove that God exists?

Phoebe believes that God exists, but she is having trouble persuading Philip to agree.

'Otherwise, where did everything come from?' she asks. 'The universe can't just have popped into existence on its own, surely? Someone must have made it.'

'I don't see why not,' responds Philip. 'Anyway, if God made the universe, who made God?'

'It's not only that,' Phoebe continues. 'How could something so complex and beautiful as life have come about by chance? Beautiful and organised things need to be made by someone, they don't just happen on their own.'

'Oh, science has worked out how natural selection does that sort of thing,' replies Philip airily. 'We don't need God these days to explain anything.'

'Well, an awful lot of people say they have experienced God. They can't all be wrong, surely?'

'Yes, they can,' retorts Philip. 'And in any case, different religions believe in different gods. So, most religious people believe wrong things which ever way you look at it.'

*   *   *

Who is right? Must God exist, as Phoebe claims? Or can we explain all the facts about the world without needing any such being? When you have thought about this problem carefully, turn to the next page.

Must God exist? Or can we explain all the facts about the world without needing any such being?

Phoebe uses three arguments to try and convince Philip, all of which have been used by philosophers in the past.

The first cause argument

The Christian philosopher **Thomas Aquinas** developed this argument in the 13th Century.

When we look at the world, we see events produced by causes. For example, a billiard ball starts to move (an event) when it is hit by another one (the cause). Each cause is itself produced by an earlier cause, and so on backwards in a sequence called **the cause and effect chain**.

Now, said Aquinas, this cannot go on backwards for ever. There must have been a **first cause** which started the whole thing off but was not caused by anything earlier. This **uncaused cause** is God. And the first event, which God causes, is the creation of the universe.

This is what Phoebe means when she says that the universe cannot have popped into existence on its own – God must have made it.

Phoebe may be right. But she believes in a God who has always existed without being made by anything else. And, if you can have a God like this, why cannot you have a universe which has always existed without being made by anything else? Both seem to be equally impossible.

So, philosophers – even ones who do believe in God – do not think this argument proves God's existence.

The argument from design

William Paley, an English philosopher, developed this in 1802.

Imagine you are walking along a beach and you come across a watch (an old-fashioned mechanical watch with hands and springs and cog wheels used to tell the time) lying on the sand. Would you think that the watch had been formed by chance, or that it had been designed and made by an intelligent being? Obviously the second of these possibilities.

Well, said Paley. The world we see around us is a much more complicated mechanism than the watch. Think about all the cells in your own body or in the leaf of a plant, each cooperating to make their organism work properly. So, it is much more likely that the universe was designed and made by an intelligent being – God – than that it arose by chance.

There are three problems with this argument.

Philip points out the first. **Natural selection** is a powerful biological theory which explains how the complicated mechanisms inside organisms can arise simply by chance. This theory was unknown in Paley's time, and it has since undermined his argument.

Second, yes, the world is full of complex *patterns* – like the beautiful structure of a snowflake, for example. But patterns are not necessarily *designs*. They may arise by chance without any intelligent being making them.

Third, the world is full of ugliness and suffering as well as beauty and goodness. So, if God made the world, it suggests God is not the completely good and loving being that most religions believe in.

So, once again, philosophers – even ones who do believe in God – do not think this argument proves God's existence.

The argument from experience

Phoebe's third point is that lots of people believe they have experienced God for themselves, and they cannot all be wrong.

But Philip is correct that different people claim to have experienced different types of God, so they cannot all be right. Does experience prove the existence of the God of Christianity, for example, or the slightly different God of Islam, or the many gods of Hinduism? They cannot all exist in the form that their followers claim.

Carl Jung (1875 – 1961) gives an alternative explanation for religious experiences like this. He suggests that, when a religious person thinks they are experiencing God, they are actually experiencing their own **unconscious** minds. It is impossible to decide about this possibility one way or the other.

So, yet again, philosophers – even ones who do believe in God – do not think religious experience *proves* God's existence.

*   *   *

So, does God exist, as Phoebe claims? Maybe so and maybe not. But many hundreds of years of thought by philosophers has failed to settle the question one way or the other.

Three extra questions for budding philosophers

Here are some related puzzles with which to test your friends, family, and teachers. There are some hints about them in the Commentary at the back of the book.

1. If God did make the world, what does the world tell us about God?

2. Our language is designed to describe objects in the world. So, if God exists, is it possible to say anything true about him (or her, or it)?

3. Scientists think our universe started about 13.7 billion years ago with an event called the Big Bang. What caused the Big Bang?

Further research online

You can find out more about philosophy and the existence of God by starting here and following the links:

https://en.wikipedia.org/wiki/Existence_of_God

COMMENTARY FOR PARENTS AND TEACHERS

1. Zhuangzhi and the butterfly

'I think, therefore I am' is the most famous saying in the whole of philosophy. It means: because I am thinking about the issue of my existence, I must exist.

Descartes was concerned that maybe nothing at all is certain. Because the evidence of my senses can be doubted, the outside world may be nothing like it appears or may even not exist at all. So, can I even doubt my own existence? No, because *something is doing the doubting*. There is one, certain fact I can be sure of: my own existence.

That seems true. But philosophers have questioned Descartes' argument in two ways:

- We use reason to reach this conclusion. But what if my reason cannot be trusted, just as my senses cannot be trusted? Then I am lost. And there have been occasions in the past when truths that seemed obvious to my reasoning later turned out to be false.

- Descartes has not proved that there is some "I" doing the thinking. He has only shown that thinking is going on, not who is doing it.

So, despite Descartes, perhaps nothing at all is certain.

1. If you cannot trust your senses, how do you know the world outside your head exists at all?

Unfortunately, you do not. It is just possible that you are a disembodied brain into which an evil demon is feeding electrical impulses which make it experience a world which is not there. Unlikely, but possible – as in the film *The Matrix*.

117

According to biologists, the brain interprets electrical impulses coming from your sense organs to create the world you see. You have no contact with the world directly, so have no way of checking whether the world is as it appears to you.

2. Can a person who has been blind from birth dream in pictures?

Philosophers disagree about how creative the human mind is. Some say that our minds merely rearrange images that come from our senses to make new combinations, rather than being able to make up entirely new images from scratch. In that case, if you have never seen anything at all, your mind cannot create the idea of visible images. Others believe the mind is more creative than that and can make anything up from scratch.

3. If you dream about a blue sky, does it mean that "blue" must exist in the real world outside your dream?

The first group of the same philosophers argue that you must have experienced "blue" before, or you could not rearrange it to create the idea of a blue sky – so yes. The second group think the mind is more creative than that, in which case it is not certain that "blue" exists outside your mind.

2. The colour blue

Experience is something that goes on inside our heads and which only we can have. We cannot share anyone else's experience, although we can guess what it might be from what they say about it. Philosophers say that experience is **subjective** – it is something that happens to the subject – the person themselves.

The world outside our heads, assuming it is really there, is **objective** – it consists of objects which everyone can see and touch.

This objective world is detected by our sense organs: our eyes, ears and so on. Contact with its objects stimulates our sense organs, which generate electrical impulses that travel down nerves to the brain. When these impulses arrive, the brain interprets them to create a picture of the world outside our heads. This picture of the world is part of our experience.

It is crucial to realise one key fact: *what we experience is our experience – not the objective world itself.* We *hope* our experience is *like* the objective world outside us, but we cannot be sure.

Now, the radiation of wavelength 0.000465 millimetres which Philip talks about is part of the objective world outside our heads. The colour blue is part of our experience.

Experiments show that most people, when exposed to radiation of this wavelength, report an experience of the colour blue. So, scientists have fallen into the habit of saying that blue light is light with that wavelength. That is not strictly true, but we know what they mean. They mean that light of that wavelength generates an experience called "blue" by most English-speaking people.

If you think that account is confusing and alarming, you are not alone! But most philosophers and scientists would agree with it.

*   *   *

The description of how we learn language through pointing, explained in the puzzle, is taken from Ludwig Wittgenstein's *Philosophical Investigations* (1953) one of the most influential philosophy books of the 20th Century. Any parent with young children will recognise the process – I certainly remember it with mine.

It follows from the above that children will learn to call "blue" whatever it is they experience when exposed to light of 0.000465 millimetres. Whether this is "the same" as the experience of other people – whether people experience colours in the same way – we cannot tell.

We can study the electrical activity going on in the brains of different people when they are exposed to light of the same wavelength. But this electrical activity is part of the objective world, not the subject's experience. We may guess that people with the same brain activity have the same experience of colour, but it must remain just that – a guess.

1. A colour-blind person finds it difficult to tell red from green. Do we know how they experience these colours?

Yes and no. We do not know how they experience either colour. But we do know that their experience of both is similar because they confuse them.

2. How would you explain "blue" to a person who was born blind and had never seen anything at all?

With difficulty! You might resort to metaphors, like this. 'You know there are different sorts of taste? Well there is another experience called sight with different flavours too. These flavours are called colours, and blue is one of them.'

3. Some people like blue more than red, and vice versa. Is this because they are seeing the colours differently?

Quite possibly – we have no way of knowing.

3. Types of truth

Most people think that a "true" statement is one that corresponds to the way the world is. But, as the discussion shows, this only works for some statements, not others.

The theory of truth which deals best with each of the five extra questions is suggested below.

1. The Mona Lisa is a great work of art.

Perhaps the consensus theory. Art experts generally agree about the Mona Lisa's greatness, and if they changed their minds (which they might) it would no longer hold pride of place in the Louvre.

Note that only the relevant experts need to agree in this case, not everybody. See further Puzzle 12.

2. Stealing is wrong.

Perhaps, again, the consensus theory of truth. Because it is generally agreed that stealing is wrong, stealing is wrong.

Society's views on right and wrong change over time. Think about attitudes to slavery and women's rights 300 years ago and now. The consensus theory deals with this elegantly – it suggests that slavery and the subordination of women were not wrong 300 years ago, but that they are now.

3. Dolphins are mammals

Biological classification (putting organisms into groups) is more a matter of putting order into chaos than finding groups which are there, objectively, in the world. Biology currently groups all animals which suckle their young on milk into the category Mammals. But it does not need to, and it may change its mind in the future. Biological classification has, in fact, changed alarmingly over the last few decades.

Given this, the pragmatic theory of truth is the most appropriate in this case. Grouping animals like this helps biologists deal successfully with the world, whether it reflects something which is "really" there or not.

4. According to Christianity, Jesus is the Son of God.

Even for Christians, 'Jesus is the Son of God' is not true in a literal correspondence sense – they do not believe that God provided the sperm to form him, or that half of his chromosomes were divine. They mean something else.

It is tempting to understand the statement in a pragmatic sense. Trusting this statement leads (Christians find) to liberation and peace. In other words, it is true because it works.

However, many theologians disagree with this interpretation!

5. Daffodils are yellow.

Is this true in a correspondence sense because it corresponds with the way the world is? Or in a consensus sense, because everyone has learned to call the experience of looking at a daffodil "yellow" (see further Puzzle 2.) Good question!

4. Tricky triangles

There are two different forms of reasoning called induction and deduction.

With **induction**, you start with some **observations** of the world and try to work out a rule or law which explains them. For example, you might measure the distances falling objects travel over different amounts of time and try to work out a law of motion which explains such results. Here you work *from the observations* of the world *to the rule*.

With **deduction**, you start with some given, assumed, rule called an **axiom**, and you work out its consequences. Here you work *from the rule to the observations* it predicts.

Maths works by deduction, not induction. It starts from a small set of axioms – such as that the shortest distance between two points is a straight line – and works out the consequences of these axioms. You will have suffered this at length while doing geometry in maths lessons at school!

Science works by a combination of the two approaches. Many people assume it starts from observations and logically works out their explanation in terms of a law of nature. But this is not so. It starts with an inductive *guess* as to what the relevant law of nature might be, works out the consequences of such a law by deduction, and then does experiments to test whether these consequences really occur.

For example, a physicist might *guess* that the distance fallen by an object depends upon the time of falling squared. He or she then uses

122

this rule to deduce that, if it falls 2 metres after 1 second it should fall 4 metres after 2 seconds, and then tries it out to see if this is so.

Scientific laws are subject to falsification – to the discovery of some observation in the future which disproves them. Mathematical truths, for example about the angles in a triangle, are not subject to falsification by observation because they are not based upon observation in the first place.

1. How can we be certain that the sun will rise tomorrow morning?

We cannot be certain of this. The rule 'the sun rises every morning' is an inductive guess based on observations that it has always happened so far. But it is open to falsification by a new observation – one day when the sun does not rise.

See further Puzzle 15.

2. Try to prove that the shortest distance between two points is a straight line.

You cannot. It is an assumed axiom of maths that is not based on any other rule or on observations. You must just accept it – or work out a whole new form of maths in which this rule does not occur.

Interestingly, in Einsteinian physics, space becomes curved close to very massive objects like stars. So, in this instance, the shortest distance between two points is a curve rather than a straight line.

3. If science has been wrong in the past, why should we believe what scientists say today?

It depends on what you mean by "wrong". Science's picture of the universe does change dramatically from time to time, it is true. But its ability to predict events and control the world does still get better and better over time. So, today's scientists may not be completely right, but they are at least almost right.

See further Puzzle 16.

5. What is a game?

Words can easily mislead us. Because we use the same word "game" for patience, rugby, chess, charades, and prostitution, this misleads us into thinking there *must* be something common to all five which the word describes. But there is not. Wittgenstein regarded himself as doing "therapeutic philosophy" – trying to cure us of fallacies like this one, rather as a doctor cures a patient.

Wittgenstein traced this particular fallacy back to the Ancient Greek philosopher Plato and his theory of **forms**. Consider the variety of objects called "tables". Plato believed that there is an "ideal table" or "form" of tables in the heavenly realms which defines what a table is. All objects which partake of the essence of this heavenly table are, in fact, tables, and are correctly called so. Those objects which do not partake of this essence are not tables at all.

It is this theory, or anything like it, which Wittgenstein denies.

1. A child learns the meaning of the word "cat" by someone pointing at a cat and saying 'Cat!' So, how does the child know that this word does not mean "pointing" or "finger" or 'Be careful!'?

The child does not know but proceeds by trial and error. For example, imagine the child misunderstands the word to mean a finger. It might hold up a finger, or point at a dog, and say 'Cat!' It works out from reaction of its audience that it has misunderstood the meaning of the word. If it points to a cat and says 'Cat!', the positive reaction of its audience reinforces its learning.

That being said, young children are at the **preoperational stage** of development, as described by the psychologist **Jean Piaget**. This means they are focused on objects rather than abstract ideas. So, they are likely to assume that single words refer to concrete objects like cats, rather than abstract ideas such as "pointing" or "danger".

2. If Wittgenstein is right, can you ever say exactly what you mean?

Wittgenstein changed his mind about this.

124

In his first book, *Tractatus Logico-Philosophicus* (1921), he argued that words have a one-to-one correspondence with objects in the world. If this is so, descriptions can be clear and unambiguous.

In *Philosophical Investigations* (1953) he denied this. All language is metaphorical, he now argued. It describes things by suggesting they are rather like (but not completely like) something else.

For example, consider the sentence 'The sun was a big orange hanging above the horizon.' Metaphors link two objects together, here "sun" and "orange" because they share only some features. So, they are not precise. Does the writer mean the sun has peel and pips like an orange, or has a crinkly surface, or an orangey smell, or is the same size, or has an orange colour? It is not clear.

Most philosophers now accept that Wittgenstein was closer to the truth about language in *Investigations* than in *Tractatus*.

   3. Can war be a game?

You can call it that if you so choose. To do so is to point out it shares certain features with other games, for example tactics, winning and losing, chance, and so on.

6. Why is murder wrong?

Although many philosophers accept the is/ought distinction, a whole tradition of ethics, **natural law** ethics, rejects it.

Natural law philosophers believe our happiness as human beings comes from being in harmony with nature rather than opposing it – "nature" here meaning both our own human nature and the universe as a whole. They argue things like:

- Because our teeth are capable of dealing with meat (like carnivores) as well as plants (like herbivores) it is right for human beings to have a mixed diet rather than being vegan or vegetarian.

125

- Because human beings are defined by the use of language, and because language depends upon agreeing the meaning of words, telling the truth is right and lying is wrong.

The Roman Catholic Church makes extensive use of natural law arguments, for instance in its condemnation of artificial birth control and homosexual sexual acts.

Philosophers who accept Hume's distinction find it very handy for attacking moral beliefs they disagree with. Mind you, they are generally careful not to let it question their own!

1. Does Hume's argument apply to all matters of right and wrong, or just to murder?

To all matters of right and wrong – there is nothing special about murder.

2. If we abandon the idea that murder is wrong, the human species might die out. Does that make murder wrong?

There are a set of philosophers called the Rule Utilitarians. Like all Utilitarians, they believe that the right thing to do is what brings the best results. Assuming that the survival of our species is a good thing, this makes the rule 'Don't murder!' a good one to follow most of the time. However, there may be exceptional cases when murder might give a better result. For example, murdering a serial killer to stop him or her killing even more other people might be the right thing to do if the police cannot catch them first. So, the rule against murder is not an absolute rule.

On the other hand, you could argue that the extinction of our species, although certainly unfortunate, is not sufficient justification for breaking fundamental moral rules.

3. Does 'Being kind is good' just mean 'Hooray for kindness!'? If not, what else does it mean?

It could mean: 'I believe it is objectively right to be kind and objectively wrong to be cruel.' Some philosophers – such as Kant, see Puzzle 7 – argue that moral principles are just as real as the "facts" which Hume talks about, even though they cannot be deduced from such facts.

Or it could mean: 'Everyone agrees that kindness is good, so it is good.' This works if you accept the consensus theory of truth for ethics – see Puzzle 3.

Or it could mean: 'If people are kind, it produces the sort of society I want to live in.' This works if you accept the pragmatic theory of truth for ethics – again see Puzzle 3.

7. Doing bad things to get good results

The biggest divide in ethics is between the Utilitarians and the Kantians.

- Utilitarians say that only the **consequences** of actions really matter. These consequences may be good or bad, and the best type of consequence is the greatest amount of happiness for the greatest number of people. For these philosophers, the "right" thing to do is simply the action that brings about the best consequences; it has no other meaning. The nature of the action itself, and the intention with which it is done, are irrelevant.

- Kantians say that the consequences of an action are irrelevant for deciding whether that action is right or wrong. Only the nature of the **action** itself, and the **intention** with which it is done, are relevant.

These two types of philosopher have opposite positions, with little ground for compromise.

Both systems have their weaknesses. Utilitarians are prepared to do unspeakable things to innocent people to bring about more happiness for the rest, which may strike us as unjust. Kantians approve of well-intentioned bunglers, who mean well but are incompetent at bringing about good results.

The Just War position is a fudge between these two extreme systems which includes elements of both. It originated in the ancient world, was refined in Christianity and Islam in the west, and is accepted by most modern western states and the United Nations – at least in theory.

The Just War position has two key parts:

- *Jus ad bellum*, or "justice in going to war". This principle is utilitarian. It says that a nation should only go to war if the outcome will be better than not doing so. Among other things, this rules out going to war if you are certain to lose.

- *Jus in bello*, or "justice in warfare". This principle is Kantian. It rules out the deliberate targeting of non-combatants, the use of torture, and unnecessarily cruel methods such as the use of poison gas, even if these would make victory more likely.

1. You cannot trust a Utilitarian philosopher to tell you the truth. Why not?

Because they do not think that lying is wrong. They will do whatever is needed to bring about the best result, as they see it. This includes lying to you if necessary.

2. The Second World War was ended by dropping atomic bombs on Hiroshima and Nagasaki. Would a Just War philosopher approve of this?

No. It involved the deliberate targeting of civilians, so breached the Kantian principle of *jus in bello*.

The Americans used the atomic bombs to shock Japan into surrender, avoiding the need to fight their way up the Japanese mainland. This almost certainly saved more soldiers' lives than the civilian lives lost at Hiroshima and Nagasaki. The Americans reasoned as Utilitarian philosophers and overruled the Kantians in this case.

128

3. What should Utilitarians do when they cannot predict the consequences of their actions?

Rule Utilitarians (a subset of the Utilitarians – see Puzzle 6) say you should follow normal moral rules, such as 'Don't kill!' and 'Don't steal!' unless it is *clear* this would lead to a worse result. It is not clear in this case, so they would obey the normal moral rules.

Rule Utilitarians argue that conventional rules encode what *usually* leads to the best results in the long run. So, it is sensible to follow them unless there is a clear reason not to do so.

8. The lifeboat dilemma

The lifeboat dilemma raises several fundamental questions about the meaning of life and our relationships with other people.

First, is survival the ultimate good and death the ultimate evil? If so, each of our lives is a tragedy (a story with an unhappy ending) because we all die eventually. If not, what is more important than mere survival? Dying heroically in a cause, or to save other people? Living a good life while it lasts? Having a good time?

Second, is every human life sacred and inviolable, or is human life a commodity that may be traded to benefit other people?

Third, in situations where we can only save some lives, what criteria should decide who lives and who dies? Chance? Age? Having responsibilities, like the mothers of young children? Those most able to contribute to society? Those with the most money? This question arises regularly in the NHS, which does not have the resources to treat everyone who needs it with the most expensive drugs and procedures. So, some are left untreated.

A related problem imagines an *over-loaded* lifeboat after a ship has gone down. There are still people in the water, but to take any more aboard the lifeboat means it will sink and everyone will die. This has given rise to a tradition of thinking called "lifeboat ethics", which argues that those in the lifeboat should save themselves and let the others drown.

This tradition likens the modern world to an overloaded lifeboat. The world is over-populated, and the environment cannot sustain the number of people currently alive at a western standard of living. So, should the nations of the affluent west leave peoples of the less-developed nations to founder, or should they help them? Helping them may result in the environment being overwhelmed and almost everyone dying, while leaving many people to die could avoid this problem. Should we consider only the welfare of people in our own nation, or of everyone worldwide?

Philosophers disagree on all these issues, as do other people.

1. In the lifeboat dilemma, should the others be willing to kill even a volunteer?

It is a noble thing to offer to die to save your friends. But should your friends, while grateful for your heroism, decline your offer? That depends upon whether they see their own survival as the ultimate good and their own deaths as the ultimate evil.

2. An evil dictator is killing lots of innocent people in his country. Would it be right to assassinate him?

Just War theorists and Utilitarians would argue "yes". Pacifists would argue "no". See further Puzzle 7.

This issue arose acutely during the Second World War. Plots on Hitler's life were hatched by his fellow-Germans, most famously one joined by the Christian pastor Dietrich Bonhoeffer who was executed after the plot failed.

3. Killing one person – a murderer – might save ten others by donating his organs. Should he be killed?

Utilitarians might be tempted to do this, Kantians would not. See further Puzzle 7.

If you decide to use the murderer in this way, you have decided that he (or she) has forfeited the right to count as a proper human being. But once you decide this for some people, where do you draw the line? Rapists? Mentally defective people? The senile? Those with whose politics you disagree?

9. Do all species matter?

In 1981, the Australian philosopher Peter Singer published a book called *The Expanding Circle*. He pointed out that, over the course of human history, the circle of those we regard as proper people worthy of consideration has expanded.

Originally, this charmed circle included only the members of our own tribe or village. At this stage, you could do what you liked to anyone else (including killing them), but strict rules governed how you should behave towards the members of your own group. No contradiction was felt about this, because humans outside the group were not regarded as proper people. Thus, the head-hunters of Borneo might happily cook and eat humans from outside the village, while treating fellow-villagers in a thoroughly moral fashion.

Over time, the size of this circle has increased. For a while it included all members of our own nation or civilisation – but not others, who could be enslaved without compunction. The correspondence of the slave-owner John Newton, for example, the author of *Amazing Grace*, shows that he did not consider the Africans in the holds of his ships to be people, but rather the moral equivalent of cattle. But today the circle includes all members of the human species, and such racism is viewed as barbaric.

Now, argues Singer, we are caught in the middle of a continuous process here and have not yet reached its logical end. For why should the category of "person" be restricted to members of our own species, as at present? Why should it not include other mammals such as chimpanzees and dogs? Perhaps in a few hundred years people will view our current treatment of such animals with the same horror that we feel towards the slavery of earlier years.

Notice two things here:

- Currently, we see all human beings as having **intrinsic value** – as having value in their own right irrespective of their usefulness to us – whereas we feel that all other species can have value only insofar as they **benefit** us. Singer argues that some other species should be regarded as having intrinsic value as well. It is hard to show he is wrong.

- Singer distinguishes between "human" and "person" and argues that the latter is the important category in ethics. A "person" is a conscious being with whom it is possible to communicate, so some adult chimpanzees are more fully persons than some human beings.

1. Is it wrong to eradicate microorganisms which make us ill, or poisonous snakes which can kill us?

There is a difference between other organisms which are simply no use to us and those which actively attack and kill us. The law allows us to harm other human beings in self-defence if there is no alternative, so should not the same apply to other species?

However, the "if there is no alternative" clause needs to be considered carefully.

2. If there are several similar species in the world, does it matter if just one of them dies out?

That depends upon whether you regard the species as having intrinsic value (in which case, yes) or only having value insofar as they are useful to us (in which case, probably no.)

3. Is it ever right to cause human suffering to protect other species?

It might be useful to consider the following points:

- Are we talking about severe suffering or just minor inconvenience?

- Which humans are we considering? Strangers or my friends? Poor humans or rich humans?

132

- Which other species are being considered?

For example, my minor inconvenience of not being able to have animals killed so I can buy my wife a genuine fur coat is very different from condemning some poor African villagers to die of malaria so we that can protect their local mosquito populations.

10. A moral code for computers

The "Who counts?" section of the Puzzle summarizes the argument of Peter Singer's *The Expanding Circle*, discussed in Puzzle 9. It then goes on to wonder whether the category of "person" should be extended to include intelligent machines. This question is becoming more and more pressing as IT advances.

The Puzzle draws a parallel between parents creating a child and an IT engineer creating an intelligent robot, and hints that robots should therefore have the same rights as children. But there is a difference. Parents do not (usually) create children to be their slaves, but to be autonomous individuals. That is not (usually) why IT specialists create intelligent robots. The "creating" is also different. The parents do not completely specify the nature of their child in the way that the engineer designes a robot with specific capabilities.

As regards the three types of moral code outlined:

- The first is closest to the position of Kant – see Puzzle 7.

- The second is close to Utilitarianism – see also Puzzle 7.

- The third, sometimes seen as a valid alternative style of ethics to the other two, is closer to the moral codes of the Ancient Greek heroes and the Vikings.

As regards Asimov's Three Laws of Robotics, Phoebe has put her finger neatly on the problem: rules like these are not good at handling conflict situations. These are situations where more than one other person needs our help, or more than one other person tells us what to do.

133

Note that Asimov programmes his robots to be self-sacrificing – to put the interests of their human masters before their own. Is this realistic? Will an intelligent machine eventually reach a level of self-consciousness such that it wants to pursue its own interests instead? We are waiting to find out!

1.   *If we make an intelligent machine to serve us, is it right to treat it as a slave?*

It may depend on what is meant by "intelligent". If we mean just extremely good at calculating, then why not? But if we mean self-conscious, as we are, then it becomes problematic, because we are dealing with another person.

2.   *Is it being human that matters, or being intelligent, or being alive? What makes another being worthy of equal rights?*

See Peter Singer's argument, mentioned above. Singer argues persuasively that what matters is being a "person", by which he means a conscious being with whom we can communicate. Devotees of the TV series *Star Trek* will have no problem accepting this idea.

3.   *Is it true that all human beings are of equal value?*

"Equal value" is a tricky concept to apply to human beings and it can mean at least two different things. It can mean that human beings are all "equal in ability", but this is clearly not true. Or it can mean that, as an act of sheer will, we should value all human beings equally, according them equal respect and dignity, whatever they are like. In the first case the value depends upon something in the person themselves; in the second it is something which we give to them. The second is closer to the ideal enshrined in our own society.

11. Is genetic engineering wrong?

Is genetic engineering dangerous?

It carries some risk, of course, but then everything in life does. Risk cannot be eliminated completely: even staying in bed is risky. The

134

trick is to reduce risk to acceptable levels, and that is what "risk assessments" at work are about.

Risks can be offset against benefits, and the greater the available benefit, the greater the acceptable level of risk.

The potential benefits from genetic engineering are huge, including for some of the poorest people in the world. Genes can be engineered into crop plants to improve their nutritional value, to increase their pest resistance so less pesticides are used, and to produce their own nutrients so less artificial fertiliser is needed. These improvements can mean the difference between life and death to many people.

Is genetic engineering wrong?

Attempts to show that it is generally use natural law arguments, discussed in Puzzle 6. These suggest we should harmonize ourselves with nature, rather than trying to dominate it or control it. But civilisation is based firmly upon the control of nature, and that includes our practice of agriculture. There is nothing natural about centrally heated houses, or fields of wheat, or wearing clothes, or reading books, or laptops, or most other things we possess or do these days.

Genetic engineering sounds frightening because it involves altering the DNA which controls the nature of organisms. But this DNA has changed drastically over time and continues to do so – it is not fixed. We have altered it indirectly by the selective breeding of plants and animals for thousands of years. Today we can do it more directly, precisely, and effectively than before by genetic engineering. It is not clear why this should be wrong.

1. Treat children with genetic diseases such as cystic fibrosis.

Cystic fibrosis is the most common genetic disease in the UK today, affecting 1 in about every 2500 of babies born. Such children have a faulty gene in the cells in their lungs (and elsewhere).

Genetic engineering involves introducing a healthy copy of the defective gene so that the lung cells work normally. As this involves correcting an unusual mistake in the DNA, rather than creating something novel, few people object to it.

> *2. Make crop plants with built-in disease and pest resistance, and the ability to make their own fertiliser.*

This is discussed above. Some people object to the practice because it is carried out by large firms which sell their products for a profit. But such is modern life – most innovations are produced by firms which generate a profit. And the technological progress this "capitalist" system has produced has lifted countless millions out of degrading poverty and suffering during the last century.

> *3. Make foods which have a longer shelf life in the supermarket.*

This reduces costs for the supermarket, as well as the amount of food that is wasted. Such food waste is clearly a bad thing. In a competitive market, lower costs result in lower food prices, including for the poorest in our society who spend a larger percentage of their income on food.

> *4. Make basic foods, such as rice, with a higher vitamin content.*

The classic case is Golden Rice, a genetically engineered strain of rice with a raised beta-carotene content which the body converts into vitamin A. Vitamin A deficiency is estimated to kill 670,000 children under the age of 5 each year and cause an additional 500,000 cases of irreversible childhood blindness. Rice is a staple food crop for over half of the world's population, so this change can potentially eliminate a lot of human suffering.

12. The *Mona Lisa*

It is unclear whether beauty is just a matter of taste. We have no trouble with things like food or drink: we do not consider someone wrong because they prefer coffee to tea, or white wine to red wine. But what about music and pictorial art?

You do have to work at appreciating classical music, for example, and someone who just writes it off probably needs to be educated so

136

that they understand it properly. Similarly, learning about paintings through the study of art history can help you to appreciate their beauty. But even when you understand both composers, there is little point in arguing whether Shostakovich's 5th symphony or Bach's Brandenburg Concertos are the more beautiful – it is largely a matter of personal taste.

Philosophers generally recognise three separate areas of human experience: the good (matters of right and wrong), the true (matters of fact) and the beautiful. And there is no getting away from it – the beautiful is the most mysterious of the three.

1. Which are more beautiful, and why: human works of art or the beauties of nature?

Kant thought the beauties of nature win hands down – a glorious sunset, a snowy mountain range and so on. But then Kant was notoriously unappreciative of human art, once complaining to the Chief of Police that the inmates from a nearby prison were disturbing him with the singing of hymns! Other philosophers think our human vocation is to improve nature, rather than just admire it. Isn't a superbly crafted garden even more beautiful than a similar-sized section of wild moorland?

2. What makes a painting beautiful: its colours, its shapes, its subject matter, or something else?

Kant plumped for the design – shapes and lines – but you could make out a strong case for any of the three. The author of this book is a big fan of B&W photography, which eliminates colour completely – but then, is not a rainbow stunningly beautiful? And arguably a vista of the Himalayas is more beautiful than a vista of the East Anglian fenlands – or is it?

The more you think about beauty, the more mysterious it becomes.

3. How should we decide how much money a painting is worth?

Should decide, or *do* decide? As with everything else, the price of a painting is a matter of supply and demand. If the demand for Rembrandt's paintings collapses, for example, their price will plummet overnight.

Karl Marx distinguished between "exchange value" – what someone will pay for an object – and "real value" – how much it adds to human happiness. That is a useful distinction. Think about the value of clean water – low in exchange value in the UK but extremely high in real value everywhere.

13. What is art?

When a parent takes the first crayoned scribblings of their child and pins it up on the kitchen wall, they are doing something rather similar to the Tate's display of the bricks. They are saying 'Look! This is special!' To them it is clearly art. Although it may not, of course, be very *good* art.

Which goes to show that art is not only something produced by a special group of people called artists. Anyone may produce art from time to time. Although it may not be very good art.

But what are people doing when they produce art, rather than making dinner, tidying a room, writing a report or fixing a car? It is difficult to pin this down, and the dinner, room, report and car may sometimes, at a bit of a stretch, be described as "works of art".

Perhaps art is just something special, something which we have put extra effort into to make it stand out and be different. Even if that extra effort is just the imaginative and insightful selection of a set of bricks!

1. In 1917, the artist Marcel Duchamp purchased a men's urinal from a plumbing supplier and entered it for a New York art competition under the title Fountain. The committee in charge of the competition rejected the object on the grounds that it was not art, which provoked a controversy at the time. Were the committee right?

Not according to the managers of the Tate gallery in London. Unless, of course, Duchamp was simply taking the mickey rather than sincerely suggesting the urinal was worth looking at – which might well have been the case.

> *2. What makes one work of art better than another. What is good art?*

See Puzzle 14 for a lengthy discussion of this.

> *3. Phoebe thinks the pile of bricks is art. Philip disagrees. Is Philip just wrong?*

Probably, yes. Although he is perfectly entitled to think it is bad art rather than good art.

14. How good is pop art?

The puzzle mentions several ways of deciding whether a poster is great art but does not consider the role of art experts in deciding. The views of experts are irrelevant if the judgement is simply a matter of personal taste – see Puzzle 12. But if there is any objective element to the greatness of art, then people educated to understand art are presumably better placed to make a judgement.

Four sorts of expert regularly have their say:

- Teachers of art at universities and in colleges and schools.

- The management of prestigious public art galleries.

- The art critics of newspapers and magazines

- The owners of small private galleries that display art works for sale.

Having said that, disagreement between such experts is the norm rather than the exception, and their judgements change over time, both of which casts some doubt on the alleged objective features of great art.

> *1. People rarely agree about just how great a painting is. Is this just a matter of opinion, or are some people wrong?*

See the parallel discussion on the subjectivity or objectivity of beauty in Puzzle 12.

> *2. If a painting is great today, will it be great tomorrow? Or does this change over time?*

Fashions in art and taste do change over time, and from culture to culture as well. Having said that, prestigious public art galleries do exhibit what they consider to be the greatest art from a range of different times and cultures. So, personal taste is likely to be different from an objective judgement about the greatness of an art work as representative of its type or time.

> *3. What matters more – how much satisfaction an artist gains from making a painting, or how much it affects the people that view it?*

That probably depends upon who you ask! Most people value their own pleasure more highly than the pleasure of other people.

15. Will the sun rise tomorrow?

Hume's argument is tricky to get hold of, so consider it in this form:

1. The future has always, so far, behaved in the same way as the past.

2. So, predictions that it will behave in the same way tomorrow have always so far turned out to be correct.

3. *This will continue to be the case.*

4. Therefore, tomorrow will be like any other day, and the sun will rise as normal.

It is step 3 which is problematic. The argument needs to *assume* it to get to step 4, it does not *prove* it. So the argument fails. Science cannot prove that the universe will behave in the same way tomorrow as it always has.

It is one of the fundamental assumptions of science that the laws of nature are unchanging over time and space – that they are the same as they were a million years ago, and that they are the same here as they are in the next galaxy. It is impossible to prove this, it is just an assumption that science makes. Science believes in the existence of a well-ordered universe, while having no idea why this order should be. Mysterious!

1. Science is based on experiments using sense experience. So, can science predict the future?

Yes – provided it *assumes* that the universe will continue to behave as it always has.

2. Why do scientific laws stay the same year after year? Why don't they change like everything else?

We have absolutely no idea. And, strictly speaking, we cannot be sure they do always stay the same. For example, when one of your school chemistry experiments did not work, you assumed you had messed up. But perhaps the laws of nature were misbehaving on your bench on that day instead. How could you ever tell the difference?

3. Which matters more: security or adventure?

In 1943, the psychologist **Abraham Maslow** published what he called the **hierarchy of needs** for human beings. This was shaped like a triangle, with basic needs such as food and security at the bottom and "self-actualization" needs, like achieving one's potential, at the top. The needs near the bottom must be attended to, he argued, before those near the top become important to us.

So, if your life is threatened, security feels much more important than adventure. Only once your basic needs are all taken care of does the need for adventure kick in. But it is very easy for people in western countries, especially children, not to notice how their basic needs are being taken care of and therefore to over-value the higher needs.

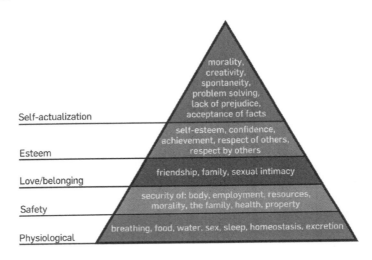

Maslow's hierarchy of needs

https://commons.wikimedia.org/wiki/File:Maslow%27s_Hierarchy_of_Needs.png

16. Has science found the truth?

Thomas Kuhn's book, *The Structure of Scientific Revolutions*, was published in 1962. Science proceeds in two different ways, he argued. During long periods of **normal science**, each discipline works within its accepted theoretical framework or **paradigm**, in this case that the Earth is at the centre of the Universe. During this time, it merely refines its theories through experiment and observation. But eventually, some of these observations put the theoretical framework under too much strain. A completely new framework is proposed, in this case that the Sun is at the centre of the universe, that the observations fit into with less strain. There follows a period of revolution or **paradigm shift** in science.

But does this really mean that science never progresses at all? Philosophers called **functionalists** argue that the purpose of science is to predict and control how the world works, not to merely describe it. If its job was to describe the world, then science really would start again from scratch during a scientific revolution, and all its previous attempts would be rejected as simply untrue. But if its job is prediction and control, then the revolution simply makes this slightly better. In this case, science really does advance, step by step, rather than continually getting it wrong and starting again. See also the pragmatic theory of truth in Puzzle 3, the theory of truth which these philosophers accept.

The form of astronomy in vogue before **Copernicus** was largely that proposed by **Ptolemy** in the second century CE. It had a stationary Earth at the centre of the universe with all the heavenly bodies rotating around it on sets of transparent, solid spheres. It was actually rather good at predicting the movements of the planets, the occurrence of eclipses and so on, even though it was based on a false picture of how the Earth, Sun, stars and planets fit together. In fact, Copernicus' theory (published in 1543 CE) took a long time to gain acceptance precisely because it did not improve astronomy's ability to predict these events.

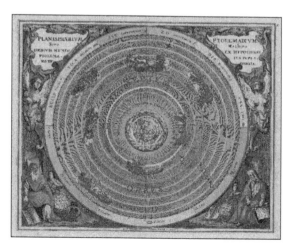

Ptolemy's model of the universe with the Earth at the centre

https://upload.wikimedia.org/wikipedia/commons/6/65/1660_illustration_of_Claudius_Ptolemy%27s_geocentric_model_of_the_Universe.jpg

Similarly, Newton's 17th Century physics is good at predicting the movement of objects, except those travelling at speeds close to the speed of light. Modern physics rejects its *description* of the world but accepts that it was almost completely true in its *predictive* ability.

> *1. The Ancient Greek philosopher Aristotle believed that objects fall down because they want to be nearer to the Earth. The modern scientist Newton believed they fall because they are pulled by gravity. Which is the better theory, and why?*

Both predict, correctly, that objects fall unless something stops them. However, unlike Aristotle's theory, Newton's uses numbers to predict *how fast* they will fall. So, it is a more powerful theory as regards prediction and control of the world. It is not, however, simply "right" – Einstein's newer picture of the world contradicts it.

> *2. According to Newton (17th Century), light always travels in straight lines. According to Einstein (20th Century), very heavy objects bend space, so light curves round them instead. How could you show whether Einstein is right?*

Astronomers observed the position of a star close to the Sun during a total solar eclipse. The star appeared closer to the Sun than it should be, suggesting the Sun bent the star's light as it passed on its way to us. This was a major vindication of Einstein's theory.

> *3. On a dark night, you can see the Moon moving across the sky around you. It looks like it is moving, and it feels like the Earth is standing still. So, why believe otherwise?*

People are often too dismissive of ancient scientists who thought the Earth stood still and everything else revolved around it. Science is based upon observation, and this sort of observation strongly suggests they were right. However, there are other observations which this theory finds difficult to cope with.

These days, of course, we can go up in a spaceship, look back, and see that the theory is wrong. But astronomers at Copernicus' time could not do that.

By Copernicus' time, Ptolemy's universe was becoming uncomfortably complex. Each planet needed a separate transparent sphere to carry it around the Earth, and the movements of these spheres were odd, because planets sometimes stop progressing across the background of stars and move backwards. Then there were the irregularly appearing comets that were difficult to fit into the system. The final nail in the coffin was Galileo's observation of the moons of Jupiter in 1610 CE.

Copernicus' theory was adopted because it made things simpler. And once it was in place, the movement of the Moon across the sky each night was explained by the Earth rotating beneath it.

17. Is time travel possible?

Kant's view is taken from his most important work, the *Critique of Pure Reason* of 1781. Well ahead of his time, Kant pioneered the idea that the world we see, which he called "appearances", is as much a creation of our minds as a reflection of the reality outside our heads. As he correctly argued, the only thing we experience directly is – our experience. Yes, we can deduce from this experience various things about the actual world outside our heads, which he called (in German) "things in themselves". But we have no independent access to that reality – we cannot get at it directly to check that our experience is not illusory.

Kant believed that "time" is part of appearances but not part of things in themselves. He believed that time is merely something our minds add while constructing the world of experience. It is impossible to prove whether this is true or not, because we cannot get at "things in themselves" directly to see what they are like.

  1. *When you are bored, time seems to go more slowly. Does it really?*

Einstein is quoted as explaining relativity like this: 'When you sit with a nice girl for two hours you think it's only a minute, but when you sit on a hot stove for a minute you think it's two hours. That's relativity.' His point was that time depends upon the position of the observer, rather than being a fixed, unvarying absolute. However, in his theory, the passage of time only depends upon the *physical location* and *movement* of the observer, not upon whether the observer is *interested* or not.

2. In the "dropping balls" case above, what does it mean to say that the two people dropped their balls "together"?

In Einstein's physics, this is the problem of **simultaneity**. He argues that the question is meaningless. From some positions it looks as if the people dropped the balls at the same time, whereas from others it does not. There is no "correct" position from which to observe the balls to get at the "true" answer as to whether they were dropped together.

3. We measure time using a clock. But how do we know that our clock is running at a steady speed? We might say: by comparing it with other clocks. But how do we know all the clocks in the world are not speeding up or slowing down?

We don't. At least, if by "clocks" we mean regular processes that we can use to measure time intervals, like the vibrations of light or the swinging of pendula. If *all* such processes get slower together, we will not be able to detect it, because there will be no unaffected processes to measure the change against.

18. Nature: guide or threat?

An interesting recent development in biology and psychology is the new discipline of **evolutionary psychology**. This explains many aspects of human minds as products of natural selection.

According to the modern theory of natural selection, animals behave as if the only thing that matters is getting their genes into the next generation. This is achieved by surviving long enough to reproduce plus success at attracting mates.

Evolutionary psychology applies this to early humans living in small groups before the development of civilisation. Success here came from high status, which generated good possibilities for survival and reproduction. Our minds have been structured for success in this setting, it reasons, and even though society has changed, our minds still retain this earlier structure.

In this early setting, human nature was a pretty reliable guide to success, success being defined as a long and well-respected life with lots of children. But in the modern setting, some of human nature has become dysfunctional, including the desire for many children. For example, whereas a liking for sweet things encouraged early people to eat fruit, which was good for them nutritionally, today it encourages over-indulgence in junk foods, which is bad for them. So human nature is less reliable a guide to behaviour than it used to be.

1. Is selfishness natural? Is it wrong?

Evolutionary psychology argues that our drives are geared to protecting and spreading our genes. As selfishness means protecting ourselves, and therefore the genes we contain, selfishness will be a powerful *natural* drive. However, some of our genes are also present in our children and other relatives, so we will naturally behave in a less than selfish way towards them.

Whether it is *right* simply to follow this natural drive is a different question, however. See the is/ought distinction in Puzzle 6.

2. Natural selection keeps a species healthy, but it is cruel. Which matters more, health or kindness?

This question may well become more pressing in the future. Modern medicine does a great job in keeping alive people who would otherwise have died young, i.e. who would naturally have been removed by natural selection. This must surely be a good and kind thing. But when these people survive to have their own children and grandchildren, over a number of generations a greater percentage of the population will need expensive medical intervention to keep them alive. Society will have progressively less resources to spend on anything else, and will become sicker, poorer and less competitive. This is the opposite direction to the one in which natural selection tends.

The 19th Century philosopher **Friedrich Nietzsche** saw this. Nietzsche flew directly in the face of most modern and ancient ethical thought by condemning the virtue of compassion – care for the weak and suffering – arguing instead for the virtues of courage, loyalty, strength and old-fashioned "manliness". His ideal was the Spartan or Viking warrior, not Mother Teresa or the Buddha. He was also also firmly against Marxist sympathy for the poor of society, seeing socialism as a degraded form of Christianity and sharing its weaknesses.

Students of ethics have viewed Nietzsche with horrified fascination over the years: fascination because of his appeal to strength and courage, but horrified because of where his contempt for the weak might lead if put into practice.

3. If we are part of nature, how can anything we do or make be "unnatural"?

We are a very special sort of animal – the first to transcend nature and control it rather than simply being at its mercy. To that extent we are unnatural. Although, of course, our bodies are natural biological systems just like those of all other organisms.

19. Magic, science and technology

Sociologists sometimes talk about the **disenchantment** of the modern world. By this they mean that everything can now be explained in terms of scientific cause and effect, while spirits, gods and magic have been banished from it. The collapse of attendance at churches and other places of worship is often cited as evidence for this process.

But human beings clearly feel something is missing in this disenchanted world and seek enchantment elsewhere: in science fiction and fantasy novels, in New Age and eastern practices, in mind-altering drugs, and in various forms of fundamentalist religion. And yes, sometimes too in magic – witness the revival in various forms of paganism in modern Britain and America.

What we have never lost is our need for the **sacred**: a part of life which is special and which transcends our everyday concerns. We may not look to the sacred for practical help, as in times past, and we may find it in unorthodox places, but look for it we do. Because the sacred is the only thing which gives our lives ultimate meaning and gives us hope in a humdrum and difficult world.

1. What is the difference between "magic" as discussed above and "magical tricks" as performed by a stage magician?

Magical tricks are just that – clever tricks. Magic is a serious attempt to alter the world by the use of non-scientific means, such as spells, rituals, charms and wishes. The appeal to magic is an appeal to the sacred for help. The performance of a magical trick is not.

2. What is the difference, if any, between a religious person praying and someone performing a magical spell?

The religious person *asks* a *personal* God (or a god) to intervene to help them. A magician performs spells or rites which *impersonally compel* an alteration in the world. Religious people sometimes use magic, of course – if they believe that saying the rosary a certain number of times will lead to a desired result, for example, or if they wear a St Christopher's badge as a protective talisman. But when they pray they are doing something different.

The Ancient Egyptians believed in an impersonal force called **heka** which suffused the world and could be manipulated to achieve results. The gods were believed to make use of the same power to achieve their goals. Magic to the Egyptians was the manipulation of heka. Prayer was asking one of the gods to help them. The same distinction still holds.

149

3. Professional sportspeople often perform simple rituals, or wear certain things, to "bring them luck". Is this magic? Can it work?

Yes, it is a form of magic.

It is impossible to discover whether or not it works, because this would need a controlled experiment. We would need to line up 100 sportspeople who use such magic, and another 100 *completely identical* sportspeople who do not, put the the two groups in *completely identical* competitive situations and see if the first group performed statistically better. Unfortunately, achieving "identical" is impossible in both cases, so such an experiment cannot be carried out.

At the very least, however, if the sportspeople believe it can work, it is likely to improve their performance, so making their success more likely.

20. The Mars colony

This puzzle raises a fundamental question. Everyone agrees that people in society should be treated **fairly**, or **equally**, but what does this mean in practice? There are at least two possibilities:

- That everyone should be awarded an equal amount of money to spend. We can call this equality of **outcomes**.

- That everyone should have equal **opportunities**, but the outcomes will depend upon their own hard work, ability and initiative.

Both solutions have their difficulties. The first removes any incentive to work hard and show initiative, so is likely to make society as a whole poorer in the long run. The latter is difficult to achieve in practice – how can you actually stop some people having more opportunities than others when they come from different families? – and means that those not gifted with ability will suffer. To simplify matters a little, the first is the solution of socialism, while the second is the solution of capitalism. This divide underlies most political disagreements between left and right in the modern world.

A modern economy involves two processes which we can (artificially) divide into **production** and **distribution**, where production is the process of creating wealth and distribution is the process of giving this wealth to different people. Our first solution above concentrates upon fair distribution of wealth, while assuming that its production will take care of itself. The second solution sets up a situation where production is likely to increase, but lets distribution take care of itself. Both have a problem with the "takes care of itself" side of things.

The UK has struck a compromise between these two extremes. It tries to encourage production by rewarding the seizing of opportunity, while using the tax and benefit systems to increase distribution to the less well off. Disagreements between the two main political parties often boil down to the balance between these two processes.

On equality, see also Puzzle 23.

    1. Karl Marx suggested the principle: 'From each according to his ability; to each according to his needs.' Is this fair?

This is an adaptation of equality of outcomes to take account of the fact that different people need different amounts of money. Some will have more children than others, for example; some will live in colder conditions and will need to spend more on heating; and so on.

The problem comes with the definition of "needs". As Rawls points out, everyone sees their own needs more acutely than those of anyone else, and we are inclined to confuse what we *want* (a large, expanding and basically limitless amount of things) with what we *need*. Human selfishness makes agreement about what each person in society really needs impossible. Hence the attractiveness of Rawls' "veil of ignorance" proposal.

2. *Who deserves the most pay and why: a doctor, a footballer, a factory-owner or a soldier?*

One solution is to rely on **supply and demand** – to increase the pay of doctors until there is just (but no more than) an adequate supply of them. But there is a seven-year time lag in the training of doctors, so this approach would lead to severe problems if applied on its own.

Most people feel that we *deserve* to be paid in proportion to our contribution to society. But there are different forms of contribution (health care, entertainment, production of essential goods, defence and so on) and no obvious way of ranking their importance.

3. *How is it decided who gets what in the UK, and does this produce a fair result?*

It is decided by a complex process involving supply and demand, the strength of the unions, historical precedent, how much people are willing to pay for particular services, and many other things.

Whether it is considered "fair" depends partly upon the two definitions of equality described above.

21. Philip's Fantastic Friends

Some animals are **solitary** and are happiest when living on their own. Robins, for example, live solitary lives guarding a territory, and only pair off temporarily to mate and produce chicks. Other animals are **social** and live permanently in complicated groups, like wolves and bees. Which are human beings more like? Can we find fulfilment best as a solitary person, like a hermit? Or are we only happy when part of a crowd of friends or a family? Or are some people (introverts) more solitary and others (extroverts) more social? The answers are far from clear.

Looking at the facts gives us no clear answer here. Our nearest relatives, the Great Apes, are social animals and live in groups. But we are different from them in some ways – perhaps in this way? We use language, and language must be learned and used during interactions with other people. But is that merely a learning phase we can grow out of to seek fulfilment on our own? Other people are sometimes a curse to us as well as a blessing; one of the famous sayings of the existentialist philosopher Jean Paul Sartre was 'Hell is other people'!

Hegel is surely right about one thing. A true friend challenges us as well as agreeing with us, tells us off when we need it as well as enjoying our company, loves us despite knowing our darker side rather than simply thinking we are wonderful. Only a megalomaniac is happy simply bossing other people around – we need to feel part of a team rather than ruler of the universe.

1. What matters more in sport, and why: winning, or having a good battle with an equal?

Experience suggests that winning after a hard-fought battle with a near-equal adversary is the most satisfying. This is explicable in Hegel's terms – the adversary we can beat too easily is not a proper person to us.

2. Why are pop idols, with millions of adoring fans, so often unhappy?

No doubt there are several reasons. But, in Hegel's terms, a fan is not a real person to the pop idol, so having lots of them does not stop him or her being lonely.

3. Theologians sometimes suggest that God made people because he was lonely. Is this a sensible suggestion?

Western theology is usually at pains *not* to see God as a large and powerful man, subject to our limitations. It presents God as the ultimate source of every good thing, completely fulfilled in his or her own right, and always acting out of pure love rather than neediness. So no, this would not be good theology.

Whether such a God exists is another question, of course. See Puzzle 30.

22. The Happiness Machine

There is surely no more important question than the ultimate goal of life. But on this, as on so many other questions, philosophers differ. The Utilitarians say that the goal is happiness, but here are some other views:

- According to Aristotle (384 – 322 BCE), the ultimate purpose of life is to achieve **eudaimonia**. This is usually translated as happiness, welfare, or flourishing and generally means ultimate well-being. It is close to one of the possible meanings of happiness.

- According to Kant (1724 – 1804), the ultimate good is to do the right thing – to do one's **duty**. Should that be rewarded with happiness, so much the better. But happiness obtained in any other way would not be a good thing.

- According to existentialists like Jean-Paul Sartre (1905 – 1980), the important thing is to live an **authentic** life. This means a life one has chosen for oneself, irrespective of the expectations of others, whether or not one becomes miserable as a result.

- According to Nietzsche (1844 – 1900), the good life is a life lived confidently **without fear**: fear of God or the gods, fear of other people, or fear of one's own fate.

- According to Marx (1818 – 1883) the ultimate good is a life in a communist **society**, where there is no private property, but where we are completely united with our own true selves, with other people and with nature.

None of these thinkers identify the ultimate good as a permanent feeling of bliss, such as we might get temporarily from a large dose of morphine. But this is possibly what Philip has in mind when he considers life inside The Happiness Machine.

Phoebe objects that truth matters as well as feelings – that illusory happiness is not true happiness at all. This is reminiscent of the position of Buddhism, which equates the state of nirvana with a totally clear perception of the truth – enlightenment.

> *1. Which matters more – developing your character, or having a good time?*

The philosophical view called **hedonism** holds that the best we can do in life is have a good time: 'Eat, drink and be merry; for tomorrow we die.' (This well-known quotation in fact comes from St Paul in the New Testament, quoting the book of Isaiah in the Old.) Hedonism may be superficially attractive, but it is alarming how rapidly good times cease to be that good, as we all know. Deep, underlying happiness is not the same thing as "having a good time", and it is not generally attained by seeking such times.

> *2. Can you be sure you are not living inside a virtual reality world right now?*

No. See Puzzle 1.

> *3. Which is better – a happy pig or an unhappy philosopher?*

This alludes to a quotation from Plato's philosophical hero, Socrates (470 – 399 BCE): 'It is better to be a human being dissatisfied than a pig satisfied; better to be Socrates dissatisfied than a fool satisfied.' At his trial, during which he was sentenced to death for questioning the existence of the gods and corrupting young people with his dangerous ideas, Socrates is reported as saying: 'The unexamined life is not worth living.' Socrates clearly would not have pushed the button and entered The Happiness Machine!

23. Can society be free and equal?

There are other meanings of equality and freedom, besides those described in the Puzzle. One more of each follows.

The Anglican Book of Common Prayer describes the service of God as 'perfect freedom', quoting St Augustine and echoing the views of St Paul in the New Testament. That seems paradoxical, because surely freedom means getting to do what I want, rather than the service of someone else? But Paul believed that God is completely wise and good, so true happiness comes from wanting what he wants for us – from surrendering our wills to his.

The American Declaration of Independence starts with this statement: 'We hold these truths to be self-evident, that all men are created free and equal.' "Equal" in this case does not have any of the four meanings outlined in the Puzzle, but means rather equality of **value**. This is the principle that every person matters as much as any other, that no one is more important than anyone else, that all persons are equally deserving of respect. This principle dictates, for example, that infanticide and the involuntary killing of the senile and the disabled should be illegal, and it is implicit in the sentiment behind the Black Lives Matter movement. This principle is not based upon the usefulness of a particular person to society. In fact, it is not based upon anything at all that can be demonstrated to be true. It is rather an act of faith, a decision, religious or otherwise, that orients us with respect to our fellow human beings.

1. Which matters more: the freedom of individual people, or the good of society as a whole?

All societies have to grapple with the tension between these two, and some compromise is always needed; neither can be absolute.

- Making the freedom of the individual absolute would lead to the destruction of society, and its individuals with it. For example, what would have happened during WWII if service in the armed forces had been voluntary rather than a matter of conscription?

- Making the good of society as a whole absolute leads to totalitarianism and misery, as in Maoist China or Stalinist Russia.

The **constitutions** of democratic states generally involve some sort of balance between the two.

2. Should people be taxed equally, have equal amounts of money after taxation, or be free to decide how much tax they pay?

156

The second would be an attempt to impose equality of outcomes, with its advantages and disadvantages. The third will not work because people's natural selfishness always makes them see their own needs more clearly than the needs of other people (see Puzzle 20.) It is not clear what "equally" means in the first case – a flat rate of tax for everyone?

The UK income tax and benefits system works in none of these ways. In 2020, the 43% of adults with the lowest incomes paid negative income tax, because state benefits received exceded income tax paid, if any. Meanwhile, 50% of all income tax was paid by the top 3% of earners. Political argument revolves around whether these numbers should be changed.

3. Should people be allowed to spend their money on private education or private healthcare if they want to?

The problem with private education is that it undermines the ideal of "equality of opportunity", to which the UK is wedded. On the other hand:

- Shouldn't people be free to spend their money on what they want, provided it does not directly harm anyone else?

- If private education were shut down, the extra pupils entering the state education system would mean considerably increased expenditure and consequent tax rises.

Unless everyone is given the same amount of money (equality of outcomes) high earners will always have more money to spend than others. So, why should they not spend it on their children, or on improved health care for their families, rather than on expensive holidays, houses, and cars? The big question is perhaps whether equality of outcomes should be our ideal, not what people can spend their money on once they have it.

24. Beam me up, Scotty!

Personal identity is a contentious issue in modern psychology, as well as in philosophy.

Some psychologists say that people have multiple mental modules, or "subselves", rather than a single "self". These modules assume control from time to time, and generate different behaviours geared towards different goals. The "mate acquisition" module, for example, produces different behaviour to the "self-protection" module or the "making friends" module. These psychologists deny that there is a "real" self underlying all this. They see a person more as an unruly team without a captain than an efficiently-run hierarchical organisation under a CEO.

Interestingly, Buddhism (which is essentially a religious form of psychology) also denies the real existence of a "self" inside people. We all change from second to second, it argues, swept along by causes and effects over which we have little control, and there is no "me" which remains the same through this state of flux.

These traditions deny that the question "Is it the same Captain Kirk?" has any real meaning. According to them, there is no "real" Captain Kirk in the first place – just sets of processes in a continual state of flux.

1. Some people claim to remember events from "former lives". How could you test whether these claims are true?

You cannot.

The "former lives" belief raises acutely the question of what it means to say that someone is the same person as a historical figure. What essence of personhood has allegedly stayed the same? The belief suffers from all the problems outlined in the Puzzle, but in an even more extreme form.

2. If someone permanently loses consciousness, are they still a "person"? Would it be OK to let them die?

Personhood is perhaps best seen as something we **impute** (give) to a being, rather than a measurable characteristic of that being. Thus, we regard new-born babies as persons, even though they are less sentient than adult chimpanzees. We regard patients in a coma as still persons, even though they are incapable of responding. And we

158

carry on thinking of our parents are persons, even after severe dementia has robbed them of the ability to do virtually anything.

If personhood is still imputed to an unconscious human being, it is not right just to let them die. In the case of someone who will never regain consciousness, however, we may reluctantly have to stop imputing personhood in this way, and turn off their life-support system. This is different from the cases of babies and very old people, whose situation is temporary.

But see also Puzzles 9 and 10 above.

> *3. Some religions teach that, after death, we go to live in heaven. Why does the "transporter" problem make this difficult to believe?*

For the same reasons as in question 1. What does it mean to say that the being in heaven is "the same" person as the one who has died? What essence of personhood has continued?

25. Does democracy matter?

Plato's (c. 425 – c. 347 BCE) key work of political philosophy is called *Republic*. In *Republic*, he argues that an ideal city would be ruled by a philosopher – a true lover of wisdom and therefore a good, just and unselfish man who is also intelligent, reliable and willing to live a simple life. These qualities would need to be instilled in him by appropriate education before he assumed rule, and this education would take until the age of 50. Rule by such a person would be superior to both democracy and any form of tyranny.

Plato is perhaps a little over-optimistic about human nature and the power of education to shape it, and also about the virtues of philosophers. But these are not charges that could be levelled against Thomas **Hobbes** (1588 – 1679). Hobbes lived through the turbulent years of the English Civil War (1642 – 1651), which gave him first-hand experience of the horrors which follow when effective government breaks down. In *Leviathan* (1651) he describes this as 'the state of nature' – a war of all against all – in which life is 'solitary, poor, nasty, brutish, and short.' Strong government is far preferable to this state, he reasoned, and the strongest possible form of government is monarchy.

1. Which matters most: being rich, being free, or doing the right thing?

These are thumbnail sketches of the ideals of the Utilitarians (provided that money can buy happiness), the existentialists (who believe that choice matters more than anything else) and Kant (who regarded doing one's duty as the best thing of all.) See Puzzle 22.

2. Should the vote be denied to people who are too young, too bad, or too unintelligent?

No democracy in the world gives the vote to absolutely everyone. This raises the question: what sorts of people should get it?

All democracies have a minimum voting age, because when too young, a person cannot understand the issues on which they are voting. Some deny the vote to people in prison, or who have criminal records for certain crimes, perhaps because they are held not to be morally good enough to decide the fates of everyone else. From time to time, educational tests have been applied as well, but this is open to abuse – it was widely used in some of the southern states of the USA to deny black people the vote, for example.

The problem is: once you start narrowing the vote down to people who are really good and who really grasp the issues at stake, you have very few people left!

3. Is Democracy just a western way of looking at things, or is it important for all human beings?

There is a lively debate among political philosophers over this issue. Is the western attempt to impose democracy on the rest of the world just an extension of western imperialism? Or is tolerating what the west sees as civil rights abuses in non-democratic states showing a lack of moral fibre?

A related issue is whether a democratic system of government automatically follows once a state embraces a capitalist economy. Marx, for example, thought that economic change automatically

160

causes political and cultural change, and is the ultimate driver of social evolution. But perhaps the two are unconnected, and you can have a capitalist economy without democracy, as China currently has.

26. The Euthyphro dilemma

Both answers to the Euthyphro dilemma seem wrong, which is why it is a dilemma:

- If God, as understood by the western religions, exists, then he must be the origin of everything. This includes right and wrong. But in that case "right" just means "what God thinks", or "what God is like". Right and wrong are not something separate at all.

- However, if right and wrong exist independently, and if God merely fits in with them, then (a) it is unclear where they have come from, and (b) God is no longer the creator of everything, so is no longer really God.

The problem disappears if God does not exist. So, some philosophers use the dilemma as a way of disproving God's existence.

1. Is it possible to imagine a universe created and ruled by an all-powerful but evil God? How can we be sure that we do not live in such a universe?

The first question implies a God who is different from the God of the western religions, because that God is defined as being completely good. But maybe these religions are correct about there being a creator, but incorrect about the creator's character? That is possible if the second answer to the Euthyphro dilemma is true. However, if the first answer is true this is impossible, because we have no independent standard against which to judge God and decide that he is evil.

If an evil God exists, we might expect the world to be riddled with suffering. Which indeed it is. So, perhaps the nature of the world disproves the idea of the good God of the western religions and suggests a less good sort of God instead?

A whole branch of thought about religion, **theodicy**, is the attempt to defend a good God against the charge of allowing evil and suffering to exist. It starts by pointing out that much of the suffering in the world results from human actions – murders, wars and so on – and denies that God could simultaneously give people genuine freedom and arrange for them always to do the right thing. This attempts to make all the evil in the world our own fault. But it is more difficult to explain **natural evil**, such as earthquakes, disease, and famines. They do not seem to be our fault, and we can easily imagine a world without them in which people are genuinely free.

On theodicy, see also Puzzle 27.

2. Who should have the final say about right and wrong in a society: individuals or the state? And why?

No society can simply allow everyone to make up their own minds about how to behave. That leads to chaos. For example, no society can allow someone to murder other people just because they do not happen to see anything wrong with it. So, in that sense, society must have the final say on right and wrong through its laws.

But there can be unjust laws: think about the apartheid laws in South Africa a few decades back, for example. So right and wrong are not simply defined by the law of the land, and the law can be criticised by individuals.

In a democracy, individuals have the possibility of changing such laws by changing the government. But that is not a complete solution to the problem, because what if the majority want a law which unjustly persecutes a minority in society? Right and wrong cannot simply be defined by what 51% of the individuals in a society happen to think. See also Puzzle 3 on this issue.

As a compromise between the rights of the state and the individual, most democracies opt for some sort of **constitution**, which limits the power of the majority to hurt individuals through their elected government. But even that is not a complete answer, because constitutions can be changed by majority votes too.

The idea of **human rights** is an attempt to get round this problem by limiting what any government can do to its citizens in the name of the majority. But these rights are notoriously difficult to define accurately. The UN declaration on human rights, for example, says that torture is wrong, and few would disagree with that. But it also says there is a human right to annual holidays with pay, which is much less clear.

3. Is slavery wrong? If so, why?

Slavery was not considered wrong for thousands of years in most of the world. In Ancient Greece, for example, the birthplace of democracy, it was considered perfectly normal, as it was in the Roman Empire. In sub-Saharan Africa during the years of the slave trade, many African kingdoms considered it a noble practice, and it was only suppressed by force of western arms after the west changed its mind on the issue.

If slaves are truly persons like us, then keeping them in slavery must be wrong. But many slave traders did not see slaves as proper people at all. So, the question really comes down to who should be considered a proper person, one to whom full consideration and the protection of the law should be given.

Over the course of history, the answer to this question has changed substantially. It used to be only the members of someone's family or tribe, then their own race or nation, and today all the members of the human species. We currently exclude sentient beings belonging to other species from personhood – chimpanzees, for example, or battery hens – and routinely do unspeakable things to them. But perhaps, in a few decades, this will be regarded as outrageous "speciesism", as bad as racism is thought to be today. Who knows? See also Puzzle 9.

163

So, slavery is wrong today because today we believe that slaves are truly persons. Whether it was wrong in the past is more difficult to answer. And we should not be too smug about our own sense of right and wrong, because future generations may judge us harshly.

27. Why do natural disasters happen?

The problem of evil can be stated in five steps like this:

    1. God is perfectly good and all-powerful.

    2. A perfectly good God cannot *want* human suffering.

    3. An all-powerful God can *prevent* human suffering.

    4. But human suffering exists.

    5. Therefore God cannot exist.

Theodicy – the defence of God against this argument – proceeds by attacking one of the first three steps. In Christianity (with a personal, male God) some of the defensive possibilities are these:

    1. Maybe God is perfectly good but not all-powerful. Maybe he is doing the best he can. He needs our help to finally overcome evil and suffering.

    2. If suffering leads to a greater good which cannot be achieved in any other way, then God might will it. For example, courage can only be developed by facing and overcoming fear and hardship. The world is thus a **vale of soul-making** where we suffer to become mature, adult people.

    3. Much suffering results from human wrongdoing. God cannot stop this wrongdoing without depriving people of free will. But people without free will are not proper people. So, suffering is the necessary price of having proper people. This price is worth paying.

None of these defensive moves are ultimately convincing, as you can readily see. So, traditionally, religions like Christianity have been forced to accept the first four steps of the argument but still deny step 5 – arguing that the existence of evil and suffering is a mystery. Belief in the existence of God then becomes an act of faith that flies in the face of the apparent evidence. Of course, such faith will only be possible if the person has had (or thinks they have had) a powerful experience of God confirming his existence. Atheists argue that all such alleged experiences are illusory.

1. What sort of good can come out of natural disasters? Does this good make the disasters worthwhile?

In theodicy, evil resulting is some greater good is called **redeemed evil**. An example of redeemed evil might be a disaster which develops the courage and selflessness of the people caught up in it, and moves other people to show compassion and help. But it is surely very presumptuous to argue that the suffering of those hit by a disaster is a fair price to pay for the development of the characters of other people.

2. Can we make *our own meaning and purpose for life, or do we need to* find *it outside ourselves?*

Where might we *find* meaning? For religious people, in the existence of God and God's plans for them. For others, perhaps in devotion to a cause, or family, or success, or to uncovering the truth about the universe. You could say we *make* meaning by *chosing* to devote ourselves to one of these.

3. Is it possible to believe in a powerful and loving God, given what the world is like?

Some people do – see the argument above. Such people who are Christians or Jews often look to the book of Job in the Bible for inspiration. Job lost everything and suffered terribly for no apparent reason, but still refused to curse God or abandon faith in him. The book holds up Job's faith as an example to us all.

28. Has science disproved religion?

Religious people can adopt a wide variety of different positions with respect to science. **Christian fundamentalists**, for example, of whom there are large number in the southern USA and elsewhere, believe that the Bible is both **literally** true and **inerrant**: that if it says the world was made in six days, this means it was, as a matter of historical fact, made in 144 hours. Such fundamentalists believe that any apparently historical or scientific statements in the Bible are true as history and science respectively, and that if modern science or historical study disagrees, then they are wrong. This is why the teaching of evolution has been banned in some schools and colleges in the south of the USA.

The position outlined in the Puzzle is more subtle than this. It realises that there are several different types of truth (see Puzzle 3), and that the Bible contains a special sort – perhaps we could call it spiritual truth – which is not historical or scientific. (That is, if the Bible contains any sort of truth at all. Many would argue it does not.)

1. Science can tell you at what angle to fire a shell from a gun if you want to hit a target. Can it tell you whether it is right to fire the gun?

No. See the fact/value distinction in Puzzle 6. Science deals with facts, and cannot dictate values – cannot tell us what is right or wrong.

2. What scientific experiment, if any, could find out whether God exists?

There is none. Scientific experiments can only discover how the world works. If God (as understood by the western religions) exists, he is not part of the world, but the creator and upholder of the world. All science does is investigate the order which God created. There may not be such a God, of course, but you cannot prove or disprove this by scientific experiment.

166

3. Should religion be allowed to stop scientists carrying out certain experiments?

Not religion as such. But certain experiments may be morally wrong, and religion is a possible source of the ethical beliefs of individuals who may judge such experiments to be wrong.

For example, during WWII the Nazis carried out a range of outrageously inhumane and cruel experiments on the interns of concentration camps. They found out some interesting facts about human physiology as a result, but most modern scientists agree that such experiments should not have been carried out.

The research activities of scientists in western universities are scrutinised by ethics committees these days to make sure that nothing similar ever happens again. The members of such committees could not stop experiments because they were against their particular religious faith. But their faith (if they have one) could inform the ethical arguments that they use.

29. Are miracles possible?

There are two different, although sometimes overlapping, meanings of the term "miracle":

- The first is that used in the headlines of tabloid newspapers. Here the term just means a very good and unlikely event, like your football team scoring an equalizer seconds before the final whistle. Miracles like this occur all the time, and they have nothing necessarily to do with God or the laws of nature.

- The second is that used by Hume: a (good) event that breaks the laws of nature, like a dead man being bought back to life when his body has been rotting in a tomb for three days (for example the raising of Lazarus in the New Testament of the Christian Bible.)

The common features of the two are that the event is unlikely, and that it is experienced as good. If a book were to fly up off a table for no reason, this would be a violation of the laws of nature, but it would not be called a miracle – the event would not be experienced as especially beneficial.

One problem with Hume's definition is that the term "law of nature" is misleading. It implies that the atoms of the universe have to do as they are told, and are rebelling against orders if they do something unusual. But what science discovers is not "laws" in this sense. Science just discovers *regularities* in how the universe behaves, which it then assumes apply at all times and in all places (an ambitious assumption – see Puzzle 15.) It is never completely clear whether science has framed these regularities correctly, or whether exceptions are still waiting to be found. So Hume is too optimistic when he says that 'these laws have been firmly established by experience.'

1. How can we be sure that today's "laws of nature" will not be disproved by science tomorrow?

We cannot, see Puzzle 16. However, they are more likely to be found incomplete, or only partially true, not false outright.

2. 'Miracle goal saves Man. U.' What does the word "miracle" mean here?

A good and unlikely event. Nothing about breaking the laws of nature is necessarily implied.

3. 'There is no testimony that is sufficient to establish a miracle.' (David Hume) Is Hume right?

In the sense of a violation of the laws of nature, yes, because some other explanation, as yet undiscovered, is always possible. In the sense of an unlikely event experienced as good, no, because we do not need anyone else to tell us whether an event is unlikely or feels good.

A final thought. To experience something as a miracle involves an attitude of mind – one of thankfulness. It does not really matter what we believe about the laws of nature, or the likelihood of the event.

It is receiving the event as a *gift* (from God, the Universe, fate, chance – it does not really matter from what) that is the key.

30. Can we prove that God exists?

Language is problematic when talking about God because *human language is designed exclusively for talking about objects and phenomena in the world.* Whereas the western religions do not think of God as an object at all, but as different category of being entirely, one that creates and upholds the entire universe of objects.

Because of the constraints of human language, if we use the noun "God", we inevitably imply that God is an object, because all nouns name objects. The western religions are at pains to point out that this is not right. To see God as a mere object, they say, even an extremely big object, is idolatry – to reduce God to the same category of being as things in the universe. This is why Islam forbids pictorial representations of God, and why Orthodox Judaism will not even use the word God at all, but at best will write G_d, because neither word nor picture can capture the divine without misrepresenting it.

It follows that, in theology, God can never be accurately described, because language can only accurately describe things in the world. All language about God must be metaphorical and allusive, gesturing despairingly beyond itself at something it cannot capture. Even the sentence "God exists" cannot be literally true, because the first word misrepresents the divine as an object, and the second misdescribes God as having the same form of being as objects in the world.

So, the best answer to the question in the Puzzle – 'Can we prove that God exists?' – is 'Don't be silly, of course not!' Because proofs use language, and language cannot capture God.

However, that has not stopped philosophers attempting the impossible over the centuries.

It is interesting to examine Aquinas' First Cause argument in the light of the above. It looks like Aquinas regards the creation of the universe as the effect of a cause, in the same way as a billiard ball moving off is the effect of another ball hitting it. But, in fact, this First Cause – the act of creation – must be a completely different sort of phenomenon altogether, to the extent that using the word "cause" for it is misleading. An astute philosopher, well aware of the limitations of human language, Aquinas did not make this mistake himself. But people reading him can easily do so.

1. If God did make the world, what does the world tell us about God?

The argument from design suggests we can infer things about the Creator from his creation, in the same way as we can infer things about the maker of a watch from its mechanism. If so, we will not infer that God is completely good from examining the creation, because the world is riddled with suffering and cruelty. See also Puzzle 27.

2. Our language is designed to describe objects in the world. So, if God exists, is it possible to say anything true about him (or her, or it)?

It is certainly not possible to *state* anything true about God – see the argument above. However, it may be possible to *indicate* something at least partially true by the use of metaphor, poetry, and similar allusive devices. Consider, for example, this passage from the Bible's Book of Psalms:

> The Lord is my rock, my fortress, and my deliverer; my God is my rock in whom I take refuge, my shield and the horn of my salvation, my stronghold. (Psalm 18.2 NIV)

This clearly does not mean that God is made of granite or metal or has battlements. Instead, it alludes to something about the help offered by the divine using metaphorical language.

3. Scientists think our universe started about 13.7 billion years ago with an event called the Big Bang. What caused the Big Bang?

We have absolutely no idea, and this question points to one of the limits of scientific explanation. In the words of Wittgenstein (see

170

Puzzle 5): 'It is not *how* things are in the world that is mystical, but *that* it exists.'

Which is a fitting note upon which to end this book.

* * *

For thirty more puzzles in the same style, see *Think Again: More Philosophy Puzzles for Children Aged 9 to 90* (2021) also by Philip West. ISBN: 978 1 8381692 1 3

Made in United States
Orlando, FL
19 December 2022

27357776R00098